To Casey + Ian

Keep stand g

defense of life! God

Bless you my friends!

Gary L. Bauer

Doing Things Right

Doing Things Right

GARY BAUER

WORD PUBLISHING

NASHVILLE

A Thomas Nelson Company

Library of Congress Cataloging-in-Publication Data

Bauer, Gary Lee, 1946–
    Doing things right / Gary Bauer.
      p. cm.
    Includes bibliographical references.
    ISBN 0-8499-1684-4
    1. Social values—United States. 2. Social problems—United States. 3. United States—Social conditions—1980–   4. United States—Moral conditions. I. Title.
    HN90.M6 B38 2001
    303.3'72'0973—dc21   2001026180
                                                 CIP

Printed in the United States of America

01 02 03 04 05 BVG 5 4 3 2 1

This book is dedicated to Carol, Elyse, Sarah, and Zachary, who are the greatest gifts that God could ever give to a man.

And to friends, staff, volunteers, and contributors, who took a chance and stood with a janitor's son trying to run for president on a platform of family, faith, and freedom.

CONTENTS

INTRODUCTION

For over a year, I fought an uphill battle to win the nomination of the Republican Party for president of the United States. For my family and me, it was an incredible roller-coaster ride of laughs and tears, elation and sadness, victories and defeats. This book springs out of that experience, but it really isn't a book about politics. Nor do I intend to lead the reader into the minutiae of Washington policy briefings and arcane debates about crunching budget numbers. Instead, I have written about you, my fellow Americans, and about this great country whose land we occupy together.

My campaign for the GOP nomination did not succeed by conventional standards. After fourteen long months, we could no longer raise the resources needed to continue. But everywhere I went during those months—and still today—Americans stopped and told me that I led them to think about our country and reexamine the issues. Over and over they urged me to stay in politics because they thought I had something important to offer to the national debate. And stay in it I will. I will stay because of you, and because I believe you deserve leaders who will speak for your values without shame or embarrassment. And I will stay because I believe America is at a crossroads, facing momentous decisions that will determine how history judges us.

When each day the morning sun breaks above the horizon of the Atlantic Ocean, the greatest nation the world has ever known goes to work. It is not mindless nationalism that allows the words "greatest nation" to slip onto this page. By virtually every measurement that social scientists and historians can conjure up, the American experiment has produced results without parallel in human history. Our military strength is unmatched, our wealth unequaled, our technology the wonder of the world. And while sound government policies have contributed to these results, it wasn't bureaucrats, policy wonks, or Washington's special-interest groups and lobbyists who made the difference. No, the real creators have been average Americans who are willing to make any sacrifice, pay any price, and work that extra hour so their children can have a better life than they had.

> **By virtually every meas-
> urement that social sci-
> entists and historians can
> conjure up, the American
> experiment has produced
> results without parallel
> in human history.**

As we traveled from one coast of the country to the other, covering thousands of miles, my family and I had the chance to meet and talk with thousands of our fellow Americans. But more importantly, we had the chance to listen. In coffee shops and suburban malls, high-school auditoriums and office buildings, in your homes, churches, and on factory assembly lines, we heard your hopes and dreams. We prayed together, laughed together, and cried together. We talked about our country's strength and the promise it holds. And we bemoaned its weaknesses and wondered how together we could make it better. It was the hardest work I have ever done—twenty-hour days, week after week. But every day was incredibly fulfilling, and at the end of each day I felt better about our country as we enter this new century.

Our nation's success springs out of the rich soil of America's families, from seed nourished at kitchen tables in inner cities, suburbs, and farms. And always behind a successful American there has been a mother or father, a teacher or counselor, a pastor or priest, a friend or mentor who reached out and gave a young person a helping hand.

I met such people all over the country. Fathers holding down two or even three jobs to pay bills and taxes and still have something left over for a son's or daughter's college education. Single mothers struggling against incredible odds. Firemen, policemen, construction workers, cabdrivers, farmers, teachers, janitors, entrepreneurs—men and women who get up early, play by the rules, work late, and do it all over again the next day. These Americans forgo pleasures now so their children will have a better chance later.

Hearing your hearts and seeing your love of family, faith, and freedom over those long days on the road made me stronger and more determined than ever to fight for your values against the cynics and naysayers. Is there greed and excessive materialism in our country? Of course there is. But there are also millions of Americans who give everything they have to help others in need. Are our kids in trouble? Many of them are, but many more are good and decent and already on their way to being productive adults who care about reliable standards of right and wrong.

In every state, from "sea to shining sea," I was reminded of old truths that had grown too dim during my long years in the brutal political wars in our nation's capital. I was able to feel again the daily rhythm of life in this great country, away from the power struggles and budget battles. I saw many problems our politicians are ignoring, more than enough to fill my heart with sadness. But I also met people whose values, faith, and spirit of sacrifice convinced me that there can be a bright future for our families, our children, and

> **The American people are better than our politics and better than many who presume to lead us.**

our country. The American people are better than our politics and better than many who presume to lead us.

> **There is a dignity that comes with work, and there is no such thing as an unimportant job.**

The headlines today focus on high-tech industrialists and entrepreneurial risktakers. I met many of both during the campaign. They deserve all the admiration we can give them, for they are the engine behind a technological revolution that is transforming our lives and the world. Too often government, through high taxes and overregulation, is making their jobs harder than they should be. But America works because of other people too—the folks who collect the garbage, fix the plumbing, pour the cement, dig the ditches, plant the crops, patrol the streets, cut the grass, maintain the roads, and complete all the other tasks that seldom make the headlines. There is a dignity that comes with work, and there is no such thing as an unimportant job. Millions of Americans hold these jobs, and for them the days are long and the monetary awards are limited. But like generations before them, they do it anyway, for their children and their future. Many of the high-tech entrepreneurs I met on the campaign trail have a picture of such men and women on their desks—their own mothers and fathers.

This book is about you more than it is about me. I intend it to be a love letter to our country, a place that has already given me more opportunity and helped me reach more dreams than I could have possibly imagined. I hope as you read it your heart will be renewed too, with a sense of the blessings a loving God has granted us and the future possibilities of this green and decent land our founders called, with hope and anticipation, "a shining city upon a hill."

Chapter 1

HEARTLAND VALUES

Virtually all the values that have mattered in my life were learned growing up in a working-class home in a tough, Midwestern blue-collar town—Newport, Kentucky. My father's bent back and callused hands taught me the nobleness of working hard to provide for a family. My mother's stoic front in the face of a life of disappointments taught me not to complain, but to persevere and grow stronger from setbacks. My grandmother took me to the First Baptist Church where I was taught the miracle of amazing grace and the power of faith. There I learned that God requires that I do justice, love kindness, and walk humbly with Him.

Grandma Gossett had endured enough pain and suffering for two lifetimes. She had given birth to thirteen sons and daughters, the last one born when she was fifty-four years old. She lost two of her sons in World War II, and another was killed when he got wrapped up in the crime syndicate that ran Newport for years and then tried to get out.

My parents covered our house with books and taught me the wonders that could be found in them, and why education was the key to a better life for me than they had. The importance of education was magnified because both of them had to drop out of high school to help their own families through depression and war. My teachers taught me that a dedicated adult—underpaid, underappreciated, and with all the odds stacked against learning—can still save a child and ignite an imagination.

> **Dad taught me patriotism wasn't a theory—it was flesh and blood and real sacrifice and pain and hurt.**

At my father's table, I learned love of country in a way that only a one-time marine could teach it. I listened with astonishment as he told me stories of the extraordinary bravery of ordinary men. He had seen things and done things in service to his country that I could not imagine. I knew the tears in his eyes when the national anthem was played were tears that sprang from holding a dying American comrade in his arms. Dad taught me patriotism wasn't a theory—it was flesh and blood and real sacrifice and pain and hurt. It was sons lost and love letters not received in time. When the flag passed by, you stood and took your hat off. On Memorial Day we went to the cemetery to mark the graves of veterans with red poppies and to shed a tear of remembrance.

The bullies in town taught me the hard way that you can't run from trouble or troublemakers—that sometimes to avoid a fight, you have to be ready and willing to fight.

I learned thrift watching my parents stretch a thin paycheck to keep a roof over our heads and food on the table, while somehow giving me a chance to be the first child on either side of the family to go to college, and then on to law school. They would sit at the kitchen table every Friday night, the meager cash from Dad's check neatly stacked in small piles to meet each obligation—the mortgage payment here, the utilities over there, money for church in another stack, and seldom a penny to spare.

Dad did everything he could to make a few extra bucks. He and my Uncle Ed sold Christmas trees one year, but they ended up in trouble because they violated the town zoning laws by selling them from our front yard. It was my first lesson in how government can hurt people trying to get ahead. I have been skeptical of bureaucrats ever since.

I collected pop bottles in the summer months to get the refund at stores and passed out grocery-store fliers to a thousand homes once a week, dodging dogs and bullies on the west end of town. Cutting grass for the neighbors earned me a little more. I learned there was no shame from the sweat of a hard day's work at an honest job.

When I ran past the old post office one chilly fall morning, the flag at half-staff confirmed that a young president had been cut down by an assassin's bullet. The tears I saw that day at home and in my neighborhood taught me that there are times when we must be Americans first and partisans later.

One summer I earned enough money to go back to college by working double shifts at the Disabled American Veterans headquarters in nearby Cold Spring, Kentucky. I filled fifty-pound mailbags and loaded them on the trucks that came and went all day long. It was a job my dad could understand—it involved muscle and sweat and no nonsense. I came home tired and I woke up sore. It was an "honest day's work," as my father's generation put it.

"How many bags did you load today, Son?" he'd ask.

"Ten trucks, Dad," I would answer, exhausted. "I worked two shifts and didn't get home until midnight." He would nod his approval.

But there was time for play too. Our family wasn't much for restaurants unless it was Huck's, the beer-and-burger joint down the street. And we never went away on vacation because there just wasn't enough money. We never owned a new car or flew on a plane. But I learned at Saturday afternoon cookouts, with bratwursts and burgers on the grill, the value of a simple meal well—talked over with family and friends. And when the evening hours came on those hot summer nights without air conditioning, I learned the power of a simple song to move hearts. My Uncle Ed, primed with a few beers bottled at the local brewery, would belt out in his tenor voice, "When Irish Eyes Are Smiling," and everyone, Irish or not, cried as if they were. That memory came back to me at a small Catholic college in New Hampshire, where the students sang "The Irish Blessing" after a long day of campaigning.

Our house, its bricks and stones, taught me something too. Mom and Dad had walked by it many times when they were first married. It was on the good side of town, the east end, not the tougher west end where they had grown up. They dreamed of buying it someday and worked hard to save up a down payment. It was kept meticulously clean by my mother, even if the furniture was not top of the line. The neighborhood declined later, and for years it was home to gangs and drug dealers. But Mom and Dad didn't budge. It was their dream home, and dreams die hard.

They had to turn the second floor into an apartment and rent it out to tenants in order to cover the upkeep. Most of the houses in the neighborhood built for single families became homes for three or four families as wave after wave of hill people came from the mountains of Kentucky seeking work and their own chance to reach a dream.

Many of the original homeowners bailed out and became absentee landlords. Others sold their homes outright, leaving in fear of crime or the gangs. But Spike and Betty Bauer hung in there no matter what came their way. When Dad would walk to the neighborhood bar every night for cigarettes and beer, the young toughs would part the way. Even in his sixties there was something about the man that said, "Don't tread on me." My widowed mom is still in that house today, and only now, after forty-three years, is she willing to concede it may be time to move on.

Dad's lifelong struggle with alcoholism taught me that choices have consequences. His cutting words when he was drunk and "not himself," as Mom would say, taught me that a child's heart can break in a thoughtless moment. Mom's struggle to keep us together was a powerful lesson that the vows of marriage were real—for better or worse. Dad's yearning to know his biological mother and father—he had been

6

conceived out of wedlock and given up for adoption—taught me the power of blood ties and the need to be wanted.

Newport taught me something about government too. The bribery, voter fraud, sleazy politicians, stacked courts, and crooked officials that caused my hometown to be known as "Sin City" showed me what happens when good people look the other way or are too busy to take government seriously. The businessmen and church leaders who cleaned up the town and, against all odds, closed the brothels and casinos and threw the on-the-take politicians out of office taught me the responsibility of citizenship, the need to speak up against corruption, and the importance of taking a stand—no matter the price.

> **I believe in achievement and success, but my hometown taught me that some people can't or won't make it, and they are our neighbors too. . . . Every person has potential, dignity, and worth.**

I believe in achievement and success, but my hometown taught me that some people can't or won't make it, and they are our neighbors too. I learned that every person has potential, dignity, and worth.

I kept all these lessons with me as I built my life and God brought me my own wife and children. The political bullies in Washington are nothing compared to the toughs of my youth. Family and faith got me through those rough streets and they motivate my political life today.

LESSONS LIVED

These lessons taught by family, church, and community have formed who I am and defined what matters most to me. Almost every decision I have made during my public life can be traced back to those years in the heart of America.

When Clarence Thomas was nominated to be a justice of the U.S. Supreme Court during the Reagan years, he was viciously smeared and his character attacked. Many of his former supporters abandoned him. Seldom has Washington seen such a vitriolic confirmation fight. But where I came from you stand with a friend in trouble, you don't abandon him. So I redoubled my efforts and formed the Citizens Commit-tee to Confirm Clarence Thomas and saw the fight through to the end.

When the GOP establishment began to waiver and forces conspired to take the pro-life standard out of the party platform, I fought at three Republican conventions to preserve it. In 1996, when presidential nominee Senator Robert Dole announced that he wanted to alter the platform, I was told that challenging him would alienate powerful people whom I would need should I ever decide to run for president myself. But it wasn't a hard decision for me. Even on the mean streets of my hometown I was taught that children are precious and a gift from God, and that the strong should always defend the weak.

When Congressman Barney Frank or Senator Ted Kennedy or Jesse Jackson attack conservative values and no one else wants to take a stand on the TV talk shows, I always jump at the chance to go into the lion's den, because you stand up to the bullies, not run from them. That's what my father taught me and I believe it with all my heart.

And when a president of the United States demeaned his office, embarrassed the country, and robbed innocence from too many of our children while the elites proudly proclaimed that private character has nothing to do with public policy, I remembered the lessons of Newport and spoke the truth. Character always matters. Private choices have public consequences.

> **Character always matters. Private choices have public consequences.**

When corporate high rollers insisted that trade with countries like China was more important to America than human rights or religious liberty, I remembered the lessons of my youth—money can never be bigger than who we are and what we believe, and appeasement never works. The nighttime stories of foreign battlefields, the flowers adorning graves at the cemetery, the tear in my dad's eye when he talked of long-ago times and men dying because of foolish politicians left me no other choice.

During my year in the presidential race, I often explained my position on an issue by saying, "I'm not going to forget the people I grew up with." It wasn't a throwaway line written by some political consultant. I meant it. I hoped it told people who were meeting me for the first time something about my priorities and about my heart, about the things I loved and the beliefs I embraced. All the things and people I saw growing up—rugged hands, big hearts, real neighbors, loyal friends, simple patriots—they were all there then, they are in my heart now, and they are there today in your hometown.

I met them day after day on the farms of Iowa, the parishes of Louisiana, and the picturesque villages of New Hampshire. America is the successful entrepreneur, but it is also the waitress raising a child alone. It's the stock market day-trader and the couple running a family business and succeeding against all the odds. It's the kid on the way to Harvard and the boy who just finished high school and is on his way to the Middle East to defend our freedom. It's the first woman who became the head of a law firm in your town, and it's the stay-at-home mom who takes care of her kids and is there for everyone else's too. America works because of investment bankers, and it works because of the guy who picks up your trash and hopes his kids can become investment bankers. It's the researcher working to find the cure for cancer, and it's the teacher who taught him. It's the cop on the beat, the fireman who will risk everything to save your house, the immigrant who waited in line to come, the mother and son floating here off the coast of Florida. It's the farmer who grows your food and the cashier who greets you when you buy it. It's the salesclerk at Wal-Mart, the pizza-delivery boy, and the autoworker. I met them all and heard their dreams, and for every minute I spent with them, I was reminded that Washington and its values don't represent America—you do, they do.

Good people still have to struggle and sacrifice. All of these people dream great dreams, work until they drop into bed at night, make mistakes, celebrate victories, and suffer defeat, and they do it all over again the next day. Most of them don't make headlines like the Hollywood stars and Washington politicians, but they pay their dues and keep their promises. They are the "American race."

> **Churchill understood that what made us Americans wasn't our ethnic heritage but our commitment to the moral idea of our founding.**

That's a strange phrase, isn't it? Those aren't my words; they are Winston Churchill's. But how can we be a "race" when Americans come in every shade of skin and our last names spring from a hundred different homelands? It isn't that complicated, really. Churchill understood that what made us Americans wasn't our ethnic heritage but our commitment to the moral idea of our founding.

Newport was settled by Greeks who made the famous sweet, hot Cincinnati chili, Italians who lived on "Spaghetti Hill," and Germans who settled throughout the Midwest. But they are first and foremost Americans. When war clouds rolled across Europe in the two great world wars, they dropped the German names of many of their streets and landmarks and renamed them with patriotic names like Liberty Alley. Then they lined up at the recruiting station, donned uniforms, and fought the good fight.

> **But average folks still know that to work hard, . . . worship your God, love your country, and keep your promises to the people you love is what makes life worth living.**

The worst tragedy that could befall America would be to run out of such people. The media elites all too often embrace the cynicism of our age. They claim that sacrifice for others is old-fashioned and out of date. They see a hidden agenda in every act of sacrifice and altruism. But average folks still know that to work hard so your children can have a better life than you did, to forgo pleasures now so you will have something to pass on to your loved ones later, to worship your God, love your country, and keep your promises to the people you love is what makes life worth living.

I'll put my faith in these "average" Americans over the power-brokers and trendsetters any day. In every crisis we have faced, from war to depression, millions of them have reached down and found the character and values to bring the country through. And I trust them still today, even with headlines and think-tank studies that suggest we have changed for the worse. They are, in fact, the American race, and they deserve a government and a culture that respects their values instead of mocking them.

And they deserve a government in Washington that puts them and their hopes and dreams ahead of the special interests, big-time lobbyists, and high rollers whose lives revolve around the getting of power and the keeping of power.

THE VALUES OF REAGAN

I worked for a president for eight years who understood that American politics is supposed to be about the American people, about their hopes and dreams and futures. I will never forget when I first "met" Reagan. I was eighteen years old and a senior in high school. It was a presidential election year, and the Republican candidate, Barry Goldwater, was about to lose by a landslide to Lyndon B. Johnson.

My father and I were sitting in the living room watching a little black-and-white television set when the regular programming was interrupted for a paid political announcement. Ronald Reagan came on the screen to give an election-eve speech. At the time he was merely a movie actor with no political experience, but that night he delivered a speech, a love song that captured my heart and the hearts of hundreds of thousands of others who listened to him.

In some ways his speech was predictable conservative ideology. He spoke about welfare reform, the need to get government off our backs, and lower taxes on working families. But Reagan added something else in a way that no one else had. He spoke about our country as a "shining city on a hill." He said that we as free men and women had a "rendezvous with destiny" and a special obligation to defend liberty. He talked about that small band of thinkers, philosophers, patriots, and revolutionaries that had formed the American nation, and he suggested their feat would have been impossible without God's blessings.

I found myself hanging on every word. His speech had such a dramatic impact on me that even today, I can, in my mind's eye, clearly see my father and me watching Reagan that night. I remember turning to my father on that cold fall evening and saying, "Dad, I think that man is going to be president of the United States someday, and I'm going to work for him in the White House."

For the next sixteen years I never lost sight of that dream of a Reagan presidency. I immersed myself in history and political science. I eagerly read his books and speeches. I was "only" a janitor's son, but I was convinced that if I worked hard enough my dream would come true. And I was convinced that if enough Americans heard Reagan's message of hope, self-reliance, and American greatness he would, in fact, someday be elected president.

In 1968 and 1972 small groups around the country tried to draft Reagan into the race for the GOP nomination. In 1976 he went all out to take the nomination from Gerald Ford but failed. Most people thought that was the end of his political career. But in 1980 he tried again. I worked for him for $1.00 a week during the campaign—symbolic pay! I had to leave a good job running the Washington office of a trade association to cast my lot for this candidate who was challenging an incumbent president. But it was Reagan who beat Jimmy Carter and ended our season of national malaise.

Later, my parents were able to visit me in my West Wing office in the White House, not long before Dad passed away. I showed him around the office and explained some of the history of the art on the walls and the furniture in the room. We looked out the window down to the green lawn below. As they turned to leave, Dad paused in the doorway and turned around.

"Gary, do you remember that evening back in Newport when we heard Reagan speak? You said you would end up here," he said.

"I remember it vaguely, Dad," I answered. I didn't want to gloat.

My father shook his head in wonder. "What an incredible country, where a janitor's son can end up working in the White House for the president of the United States!"

It is an incredible country, and I worked for an incredible president. He brought the Soviet Union to its knees and lowered taxes on families, entrepreneurs, and workers. But most importantly, he came into office and restored the confidence of the American people in our country and its institutions. The eight years that I served him were an unbelievable opportunity.

The dignity and values Reagan brought to the Oval Office have been trashed over the last eight years. Reagan perceived the office as almost a shrine, a place where presidents made decisions that resulted in our sons and daughters being sent to foreign battlefields. He seldom entered it without his coat and tie on. He told me that office didn't belong to him, it belonged to the American people. What a contrast to the events that have stained that office in recent years. Hopefully, President Bush will be able to restore some of its lost dignity.

Today Ronald Reagan and his family are suffering from the terrible disease of Alzheimer's, the same illness my father dealt with in the last years of his life. His son, Michael Reagan, has told me there are days when his father doesn't recognize him. There are visits when this incredible man, who inspired us with the power of his words, doesn't speak at all. He has forgotten he was president. It would be a tragedy, indeed, if we forget what he taught us about how a great nation ought to conduct itself in the world and at home when dealing with the weak, the defenseless, and those yearning to be free.

> **Inevitably, one morning the news will bring us word that Ronald Reagan has passed on to his reward. I know my heart will break at the news.**

When he fell late in 2000 and broke his hip, it reminded me that, inevitably, one morning the news will bring us word that Ronald Reagan has passed on to his reward. I know my heart will break at the news. Some in Washington are suggesting that Reagan's likeness be added to Mount Rushmore or that a monument be built to honor him in Washington. But the real monument has already been built in the hearts of millions of people around the world, now free men and women because he had the courage to confront Communism and call it what it was—the focus of evil in the modern world. Reagan believed that average Americans with the right leadership could accomplish anything they put their hearts and minds to. He trusted them and devoted his political life to defending their values.

For thirty years I, too, have tried to be a voice in Washington for the average guy. That is what led me to the Reagan White House to fight for a profamily policy, it is why I devoted five years to trying to reform education, and why I turned down a lucrative law career to take a decade to build the premier group in Washington that represents average taxpayers and traditional values. It is why I put everything on the line to conduct a long-shot campaign for the GOP presidential nomination, and why I would do it again tomorrow.

As I write this book I am fifty-four years old, a relatively young man in the world of politics. I hope and believe that I will have many good years ahead of me. But whatever happens, I will keep the promise I made to the people I grew up with and who built this great country. It is the same one I made on the campaign trail. I will continue to fight the good fight for family, faith, and freedom.

CHAPTER 2

THE DAY AFTER COLUMBINE

I decided to announce my candidacy in Newport, Kentucky, at the public high school I attended, to highlight my working-class background. Sprinkled through the audience would be some former classmates, cousins, and other extended family. The logistical planning took weeks: Who would introduce me, where would the press pool be located, would my shy mother be willing to sit onstage with the rest of the family, who would sing at the event, how cooperative would the school be, and how interested would this predominately high-school audience be at such an event? After all, weren't teens known to have great disdain for politicians? In short, though we planned every possible detail, this would be a day when press coverage of the campaign would be at its height, and there were still plenty of opportunities for misjudgments to mar what was to be a celebratory event.

I spent weeks preparing my announcement speech. I wrote it myself, knowing that no speechwriter would be able to capture my heart and what I wanted to say in my own words that day. Night after night I practiced delivering my speech either in front of a mirror or for my long-suffering family, who heard it so many times they knew it better than I did. I was determined to be able to give the speech without notes or a TelePrompTer, to own it in both my heart and my head.

As the day for the announcement trip approached, I grew more nervous, but also more confident about what I intended to say. I planned to talk about a wide range of issues, from Bosnia to the need for welfare reform.

> **Time and time again the names of little American towns we had not heard before have been burned into our memory—names like Paducah, Kentucky; Pearl, Mississippi; or Jonesboro, Arkansas—where American kids had killed American kids.**

The day before the trip, I left our campaign headquarters early to spend some time relaxing at home and go over my remarks one more time. After all, the day ahead would be physically and emotionally exhausting. The whole family had to be at Dulles Airport in suburban Virginia before 6:00 A.M. the next day, looking fit and rested and ready to interact with the accompanying press from the moment we arrived.

Late that afternoon I paced back and forth in my den, reciting the remarks out loud one last time. As I paced I glanced at the television; it was on, but the sound had been turned down. One look at the screen and I knew something was terribly wrong. The CNN reporter was breaking a story about a school shooting. I turned up the volume, collapsed into my chair, and along with millions of Americans, listened to the heartbreaking story unfold at Columbine High School in Littleton, Colorado.

Of course, this wasn't the first time Americans were glued to their television sets as news broke of incredible acts of mindless violence in our schools. Time and time again the names of little American towns we had not heard before have been burned into our memory—names like Paducah, Kentucky; Pearl, Mississippi; or Jonesboro, Arkansas—where American kids had killed American kids. But Columbine was clearly the worst on a growing list of the carnage of innocent children, the utter disregard for life, and the hardness of heart of the killers. The vivid images that came into our living rooms of crying American children, fearful for their lives, being herded to safety by uniformed men seemed more reminiscent of Bosnia or some other war zone than it did of America.

Later we learned that the two shooters killed twelve children and a teacher that day, before taking their own lives. Twenty-three people were wounded. The toll could have been worse. The boys had placed two twenty-pound propane bombs in the school cafeteria. Had they gone off as planned, hundreds could have died.

I immediately decided to drop much of the speech I had spent weeks rehearsing. Instead, I spent a sleepless night trying to rewrite my remarks to reflect this terrible tragedy. The audience at Newport High School the next day would be filled with parents, grandparents, and kids. Like all Americans they would want to know why these incidents of mindless violence were taking place during a period of peace and prosperity, and whether I had any solutions to offer them and our country. During my campaign, I returned to the events at Columbine many times in an effort to force a conversation about our values, our children, and our nation. I am not satisfied the presidential candidates adequately addressed this issue. Everyone bemoaned the violence, but few solutions were offered. And the solutions that were offered avoided the central moral questions.

THE POLITICS OF GUNS

According to the liberal establishment, media, and politicians alike, the problem at Columbine was guns. Many well-meaning Americans agree. Few issues cause debate as intense and emotional as this one. I saw that intensity time and time again on the campaign trail, and I saw both common sense and our Constitution being trampled in the process. This issue is personal for me. I briefly shared an office and became friends with James Brady during the Reagan campaign in

1980. Brady was shot along with the president outside the Washington Hilton on that terrible day early in Reagan's first term. The president survived his wounds with no lasting effect, but Brady, his wife, Sarah, and their family were plunged into a nightmare. This outgoing, humorous, vibrant man was sentenced to a wheelchair and constant care for the rest of his life. The experience understandably turned the Bradys into gun-control advocates and has led them to actively campaign against many of their old conservative friends. They are perhaps the most effective spokespeople for more regulation the gun-control forces have.

It would take a hard heart to not understand the depth of their emotion on this issue. Anyone touched directly by firearm violence is going to feel a natural desire to "do something," and lobbying for more gun laws must be a satisfying outlet.

In addition, there is no shortage of politicians and media commentators ready to exploit every gun tragedy and turn it into a call for more government power at the expense of law-abiding citizens. After every school shooting, every workplace rampage, and every tragic accident, the lobbying is turned up a notch and more laws to restrict gun ownership are proposed. Former President Clinton barely waited until the funerals were over in Littleton before trying to score political points from the tragedy.

There are signs that this rush for more government power isn't working. Most voters I met on the campaign trail understood that there are thousands of state and federal laws already on the books that

> **It would take a hard heart to not understand the depth of their emotion on this issue. Anyone touched directly by firearm violence is going to feel a natural desire to "do something," and lobbying for more gun laws must be a satisfying outlet.**

aren't being enforced. No one wants guns in schools, deranged people having access to fire-arms, or criminals having wea-pons. If we seriously implement current law, as we should, then our streets, homes, schools, and workplaces will be safer. That doesn't require new laws; it requires taking current law seriously.

> **If we seriously implement current law, as we should, then our streets, homes, schools, and workplaces will be safer. That doesn't require new laws; it requires taking current law seriously.**

But there is a deeper issue here too. I believe the horrifying violence in American life has little to do with the availability of guns and everything to do with our growing virtue deficit. In the 1950s and 1960s back in Kentucky, my father's shotguns rested in a corner of our upstairs hallway. The same was true of every home on the block. I did not know a family in Newport who didn't own a gun for recreation or for protection. The tough public schools I attended had more than their fair share of youthful thugs to avoid, and more than once after classes crowds gathered to watch and urge on a couple of guys settling things with their fists. It wasn't unusual for me to go to school worried about a black eye or a bloody nose. But in all those years growing up in that tough town, it never crossed my mind that another student might bring a gun to school and start using his classmates for target practice.

There were still some limits that even the tough kids wouldn't violate. The culture wasn't permeated with graphic and realistic depiction of violence and mayhem, as it is today. The breakdown of the family unit was just starting to accelerate, but most kids still had a father in the home to provide discipline. There was more of a moral consensus about reliable standards of right and wrong. Even at Newport High School, in a city run by organized crime, the school day began with prayer and every kid—even the tough guys—knew enough to be quiet or end up in the principal's office. In fact, when the Supreme Court ruled school prayer unconstitutional in 1963, the students in my inner-city high school walked out of class in protest. Some of that reaction was youthful exuberance and a chance to avoid classes, but there was also a genuine sense that something important had happened and that it was bad. They were right. Voluntary prayer and the Pledge of Allegiance to the flag sent important messages to even the toughest kids.

> **There are consequences when you tell young women they have a "right" to take innocent human life. Can we be that surprised when some young men conclude life is cheap?**

And, of course, back in the '50s and early '60s we had not yet seen the undermining of the sanctity of human life that was unleashed in the early '70s by *Roe v. Wade*, the Supreme Court decision that removed all legal protection from defenseless unborn children. There are consequences when you tell young women they have a "right" to take innocent human life. Can we be that surprised when some young men conclude life is cheap?

But these are issues the political establishment usually doesn't want to talk about. I was campaigning in May of 1999 when word reached me of a dramatic hearing on Capitol Hill that surprised the politicians. The grieving father of Rachel Scott, who was killed at Columbine High School, was invited to testify before a House Judiciary Subcommittee. Many members assumed that Darrell Scott would be another convert to the cause of more gun laws, even though Eric Harris and Dylan Klebold had violated seventeen existing laws on the day of their rampage.

But instead, Scott told the astonished committee, "In the days that followed the Columbine tragedy, I was amazed at how quickly fingers began to be pointed at groups such as the NRA. I am not a member of the NRA. I am not a hunter. I do not even own a gun. . . . I do not believe that they [the NRA] are responsible for my daughter's death. . . . If I believed that they had anything to do with Rachel's murder I would be their strongest opponent."

Darrell Scott wasn't following the script. He slammed the politicians for looking for "scapegoats" and after every tragedy passing "more restrictive laws that continue to erode away our personal and private liberties."

Then this grieving father summed it all up. "We do not need more gaudy television evangelists spewing out verbal religious garbage. We do not need more million-dollar church buildings built while people with basic needs are being ignored. We do need a change of heart and a humble acknowledgment that this nation was founded on the principle of a simple trust in God."[1]

Now there was a story. A grieving father steps out of the box Washington wanted him in and spoke truth to power. It was electrifying testimony that blasted all the stereotypes of the Washington establishment. So it shouldn't come as a surprise that not one American in ten thousand ever found out it took place. Not one national news show that evening brought Darrell Scott's wisdom to the rest of the country. He wasn't on any of the Sunday talk shows. Basically, his riveting testimony was ignored because it didn't fit neatly into the world-view that prevails among American elites today.

Americans overwhelmingly favor measures to improve gun safety and laws that keep guns away from criminals or out of the hands of those too immature to handle them. Instant background checks make sense. But I have found from one end of the country to the other a growing sense that what some politicians really want to do is take guns away from law-abiding citizens, as though the Second Amendment in the Bill of Rights didn't exist. Gun-control laws are aimed at criminals, but criminals by definition are people who ignore the law. Instead the laws fall on the backs of the weekend hunter, the single mother trying to protect herself and her children in urban America, collectors and hobbyists—people who find more and more roadblocks frustrating them from exercising their rights.

One night after a long day of campaigning in Iowa, I got the chance to see firsthand what a lot of Americans think about the constant stream of gun laws. We pulled into the parking lot of Theo's Restaurant, just outside of Sioux City, Iowa, fully expecting to be its last customers of the day. Instead we found a parking lot full of cars, pickup trucks, and even a tractor or two. It was "best buck" night, and the restaurant was overflowing with Iowa hunters, many in their best hunting clothes, there to display and admire the best racks of the hunting season. Judges examined each rack for the number of points of each antler, overall size, and weight. It didn't take long once the crowd recognized me for them to give me an earful on the gun issue. These men were angry, and they believed, with some justification, that Washington had no sense or understanding of their values.

I grabbed a chair and moved it to the center of the room, stood up on it, and began to talk to the crowd about freedom and the Bill of Rights. Soon the talking stopped and the crowd gathered around to listen. Heads started to nod in agreement. The applause started when they realized that even though I was a guy in a suit from Washington, D.C., I still understood them and their culture. Those were good men and women. We have nothing to fear from them. As hunters, most of them are practicing a family tradition that goes back generations. These are the people I grew up with. The Washington bureaucrats, politicians, and elites should get off their backs.

By the way, I did very well in that county on caucus night in Iowa, and I am proud to have done so. These folks know that America has a values problem, not a gun problem, and they decided I understood that too. Their recreational activities and their rural culture have absolutely nothing to do with what happened at Columbine. Responsibility lies with the murderers, and unless we are willing to ponder what created them, more tragedy lies ahead.

CONFRONTATIONS OF MORALITY

Eric Harris and Dylan Klebold have received an extraordinary amount of coverage for their murderous deeds. They were pictured on the fronts of news magazines, and their taste in music and diary rantings have been dissected in search of what made them into moral zombies. In an age that rejects reliable standards of right and wrong and the very existence of evil, these two boys present a dilemma to the analysts, academicians, and experts we so often hear on television.

In the hours and days that followed the shooting in Littleton, America learned a lot about the incredible clash of good and evil that converged at Columbine High. Two of America's children had become murderers, but dozens of others in the school were heroes and heroines. One boy draped his body over his sister and another smaller student to protect them while Eric and Dylan walked through the school library finishing off the wounded. When they escaped death, the boy attributed it to God making them invisible because they were praying so hard. The Columbine High School choir barricaded themselves in the choir room where they were practicing when they heard shots outside in the hallway. The frightened students laid down on the floor and put their hands over their heads. When one student asked if "Anyone here has religion," another said, "Yes," and led the students in prayer. Other students didn't want to leave a beloved dying teacher when the SWAT team rescued them. Several students were confronted by the two killers about their faith in God.

The most dramatic confrontation of all was between the boys and Cassie Bernall. The gunmen asked her if she believed in God. Knowing the boys and their involvement in dark philosophy and their hatred

> These remarkable stories of courage should, even in the tragic outcome, stir in us a sense of optimism. If our culture at its worst can produce such killers, at its best it can still create such heroes.

of God, Cassie had to know that the safe answer was "No." But she said yes, she believed, and she died for her answer. Valeen Schnurr, another classmate, was heard screaming, "Oh my God, oh my God," when she, too, was confronted by one of the gunmen, but she survived. And another young woman, Rachel Scott (it was her father who testified before Congress), stood her ground, too, when confronted by the killers. These remarkable stories of courage should, even in the tragic outcome, stir in us a sense of optimism. If our culture at its worst can produce such killers, at its best it can still create such heroes.

According to student eyewitnesses, Eric Harris and Dylan Klebold greeted each other in the hallway with the Nazi salute. Their antisocial behavior was well known throughout the school, yet there is virtually no evidence that the Nazi salute or any of the other outrages ever brought them to the principal's office. If a teacher had been so bold as to discipline them, the American Civil Liberties Union (ACLU) would have been there in a moment to protect their right to free speech. In fact, in the weeks following the shooting, when schools around the country expelled students who showed up at school in the long, black trench coats that were Eric and Dylan's signature uniform, civil libertarians dragged the schools into court. But if a teacher at Columbine had made the "mistake" of reading a Bible verse to Eric and Dylan, or suggested to them that God loved them no matter what demons they wrestled with, that teacher would probably have been in the principal's office the same day.

Unbelievably, even as Littleton parents and children tried to mourn, the religious police were on the job. Crosses erected in honor of the murdered students and teacher had to be taken down after complaints that they were on public property, and according to the ACLU and other groups, this violated the separation of church and state. Parents of slain students who designed individual murals in honor of their children for a memorial at the school were told to change them if the design included religious symbols such as a Bible or a cross. But of course, those things best explained what their children cared about the most. Such hostility to the expression of faith is not surprising in Communist China or Sudan, but it goes against everything for which America stands.

My point is simply this: No one, right or left, Republican or Democrat, wants a country with more young people capable of the murderous acts that took place at Columbine. Instead, everywhere I went across our nation, people made it clear they wanted a nation where more of our children are capable of virtue under fire. Yet, many of the things we do in our popular culture, in our courts, and in our politics make it harder for America to accomplish this goal, and events like what occurred at Columbine are the result.

Eric Harris and Dylan Klebold were exactly the kind of young men our Founding Fathers feared and dreaded the most—rootless young men who hated God while denying he existed, hated their country, despised their families, and thought life was cheap, not sacred. We have seen such men before: goose-stepping through Europe in the 1930s, running the prisons of the old Soviet Union, or rioting in the streets of the world's democracies. Such men are incapable of self-government or of tempering liberty with virtue. Their philosophy is nihilism, the exact opposite of the ordered liberty under God that serves as the foundation of the American republic.

But I do not despair. Eric and Dylan do not represent our future. Months after the shooting I went to Littleton, Colorado, and walked the grounds around Columbine. I met Cassie Bernall's brother and many other young people whose lives had been touched by the events of that terrible April day. I was overwhelmed by their optimism in the face of tragedy and the lack of bitterness toward the killers. These are wonderful kids and they are our hope for the future. All over the Littleton area I saw hand-lettered signs—in stores, in car windows, on the doors of homes, and in front yards—signs that simply said, "Let Our Children Pray." The good citizens of Littleton were doing what Americans have always done when in trouble or confronted by raw evil—they were turning back to God, the author of our liberty.

PRAYER AT NORTHERN HIGH

I thought about the courageous kids at Columbine a few months later when a high school outside of Washington, D.C., became another battleground over religion in the public square. At Northern High School in Calvert County, Maryland, a prayer had been part of the graduation ceremony for years. But in 1999, when it became known that seventeen-year-old Julie Schenk would deliver an invocation during her remarks at commencement, one student complained.

The objector was well known at the high school. The year before he had refused to stand for the Pledge of Allegiance, and when the school tried to discipline him, the ever-vigilant ACLU jumped to his defense. Already shell-shocked and fearful of a lawsuit, school officials sided with the dissenter, as did the state attorney general's office. Once again, one student's "rights" were used as a battering ram to make everyone else give up their right to free speech and religious liberty.

Julie Schenk had been taught by her parents to respect authority, and while she was deeply disappointed that she could not follow her heart and thank God for her blessings, she agreed to drop her prayer and, instead, merely ask the audience to take thirty seconds for a time of reflection. The *Washington Post* gleefully reported the "compromise," and no doubt the ACLU staff popped champagne corks to celebrate yet another victory in forcing Americans to be silent about their most deeply held beliefs.

How many times have we seen this pattern? One dissenter sets the rules. No one talks about tolerance when it is traditional values and beliefs that are trying to be heard!

But perhaps things are changing. The students and parents at Northern High School weren't quite ready to go gently into the night. On graduation night, as Julie showed respect for authority and asked for that time of reflection, a surprising thing occurred. A loud male voice in the middle of the audience of four thousand simply said, "Our Father, who art in heaven . . . " As he continued the Lord's Prayer, the members of the audience began to join him one by one.

"It started across the hall, and it picked up steam and went around the room," with at least half of the parents, neighbors, and students joining in, reported the *Washington Post*.

Audience members were later defiant with reporters who covered the story. One woman said, "I'm not a member of the religious right or anything, but I am an American and no one is going to tell me when I can pray."

The ACLU spokesman was apoplectic and quoted as saying, "The real loser here is the Constitution." Imagine, the ACLU finally saw a demonstration it didn't like![2]

I don't know the name of the man who began the Lord's Prayer that evening. Newspaper articles did not identify him either. I don't know if he planned his protest for days or if he was moved at that moment to take a stand. I don't know what party he belongs to; I don't know his race, the church he attends, or whether he lives an exemplary life. All I know is that one evening, in one community, one man had had enough, and he decided to take a stand. And I can't help but

> I don't know the name of the man who began the Lord's Prayer that evening. . . . I don't know if he planned his protest for days or if he was moved at that moment to take a stand. . . . All I know is that one evening, in one community, one man had had enough, and he decided to take a stand.

believe that a seventeen-year-old girl halfway across the country in Colorado responding, "Yes, I believe" to a boy with a shotgun, knowing full well that she would die for her answer, made it more likely that an adult man in suburban Maryland would suddenly find his voice and be willing to risk a little embarrassment to defend one of the central ideas of our country—religious liberty. And call me a fool if you want, but I believe Cassie knows what he did and smiled at his courage. As painful as their personal losses must be, I believe that many of the parents of the slain students have come to realize the enormous impact their children's untimely deaths have had on young and old alike.

I was in the middle of a hard day of campaigning somewhere in the heartland when my office faxed the *Washington Post* account of the graduation to my hotel room. It was tonic for my soul. Yes, there is still courage; yes, stout hearts still beat; yes, there is a place where Americans will stand and not be pushed anymore. Suddenly, I remembered why I was running for president.

Chapter 3

———— ⁂ ————

WE HOLD
THESE TRUTHS

I think I spent more time in school during my campaign than I did when I was a student! The classrooms of America are a great stage for a candidate running for office. The American people care deeply about the education of our children. The first two buildings early colonists erected in their small villages were almost always a school and a church! The visits I made to dozens of schools gave me an opportunity to demonstrate that reforming education would be a top priority of my administration. I loved every minute I spent with America's children and their dedicated teachers.

There were other reasons I spent a lot of time in the nation's schools. During the Reagan administration, I served as undersecretary of education, the number two person in the department. For five years I dealt with the education bureaucrats in Washington on a daily basis — ten thousand of them. I assisted Education Secretary William Bennett in administering an $18 billion budget—a budget that has now ballooned to $40 billion. We ran into incredible resistance trying to get education reform past the establishment in Washington. Secretary Bennett decided to go over their heads and visited many classrooms during those years, and I often went with him. We learned that whether it was reading out loud to first graders or sitting in on a high-school government class, America's kids are full of surprises and challenges.

In every school I visited during the campaign, I did my best to talk directly to the students, to answer their questions about government and politics and about why I was running. Among the younger children the questions were often about my own children—how old were they, what did they like in school, did I miss being with them when I was campaigning? In those classrooms I was often asked if I would promise not to lie if I were elected president—a promise I gladly made! When I was growing up, most American children associated the presidency with the truth. I remember being taught in the first grade about George Washington and the cherry tree. But today, with everything that has been in the headlines, tragically, our children have come to associate the Oval Office with lying! Many years ago, President John Adams wrote a prayer to his wife. The words are inscribed on the marble mantelpiece of the State Dining Room in the White House, where I read them many times when I worked there with President Reagan: "May none but honest and wise men ever rule under this roof." Hopefully, someday our children will again believe that is true.

Spending time with the younger elementary children was fun, but it was with the older high-school students that the questions were most provocative and challenging. Many candidates, fearing tough questions, don't risk question-and-answer sessions with teenagers—there's too much chance of embarrassment. And given political history, I avoided spelling contests at all costs! But I always looked forward to any day when I had a chance to talk directly to the kids who represent America's future. If you can't deal with American teenagers, how can you expect to deal with foreign policy or other tough issues that require strong leadership?

REFORMING THE SYSTEM

During my travels I also met scores of principals and teachers, dedicated men and women who are devoting their lives to teaching the rising generation. Many of them teach in spite of great financial sacrifice for themselves and their families. It wasn't unusual to meet teachers who bought their own classroom supplies to make up for the lack of resources supplied by the school district. The country is spending more on our schools today than ever before, but too little of it makes it

> **The country is spending more on our schools today than ever before, but too little of it makes it to the teachers and students for whom it was intended.**

to the teachers and students for whom it was intended. Part of the problem is bureaucracy—not only in Washington, D.C., but at the state and local levels too. We have more overhead and education bureaucracy than ever before, and it frustrates parents and taxpayers.

I also learned enough in those years to be totally committed to reform of our schools. Our education system is bedeviled with problems that result in some children, overwhelmingly poor and minorities, being left behind with no real chance of entering the economic mainstream. All over the country I met parents willing to make incredible sacrifices to get their kids out of schools that aren't working. I met teachers willing to go outside the lines to help kids make it. I talked to volunteer tutors, urban pastors, and local reformers all making extraordinary efforts to rescue kids.

One possible solution—not a panacea, but a step in the right direction—would be to bring more choice into the system through vouchers and tax credits. But every attempt to give low-income parents more opportunity for their children has been blocked, not by conservatives, who are constantly attacked for not caring about the poor, but by the liberal establishment. Powerful teachers unions, leading liberal politicians, and urban bureaucrats dig in their heels and spend massive amounts of money to block choice proposals.

The hypocrisy is unbelievable. Urban public school teachers send

> **The hypocrisy is unbelievable. Urban public school teachers send their own children to private schools at twice the rate of the general population, while their unions block the same choice for other parents.**

their own children to private schools at twice the rate of the general population, while their unions block the same choice for other parents. For twenty years, successive Congresses have blocked every attempt to provide education choice, but 26 percent of House representatives and 41 percent of senators send their own children to private schools. These elected officials are prosperous compared to the general public and are thus able to get better alternatives for their children, while doing everything they can to make sure their children are not in a class with poorer or minority students.[1]

The current system is neither just nor fair. Too many children are being hurt. The entrenched interests are winning for now, but their day is up and change is coming. I am convinced of it.

FOUNDING PRINCIPLES

Some of the problems I saw go deeper than money or bureaucracy. We have less of a consensus today on what every American child should know about our country, our history, and our values. In some classrooms, political correctness prevails over history. We use valuable classroom time for everything from sex education to trendy electives, while requiring fewer hours on the basics—math, science, history, and English. One national study says American students can't name one Supreme Court justice or their own senators or congressmen, but they have detailed knowledge of the members of the latest rap or hip-hop group. Incredibly, during the heated 2000 presidential race, many teenagers in one study couldn't name the vice presidential running mates of either George Bush or Al Gore. During President Bush's inauguration, one protester held up a sign that read, "Abolish the Electrical College." Whatever you think of the Electoral College, our schools do need reform!

On one of my first school visits, to a high school in Minnesota, I began to see firsthand what our children are missing. I toured the beautiful building amazed at the resources this fortunate suburban school enjoyed. There were computers widely available, up-to-date science labs, and new textbooks. In a small auditorium I met with a couple hundred students. I made a brief presentation of why I was running for the Republican presidential nomination. The students listened politely, but I could see most of them were distracted. A big football game was coming up the next day, and no doubt the thought of beating a cross-town rival was foremost in their minds. I needed a gimmick to spark their interest. Our daughter Elyse had given me an idea just before my presentation, and I decided to try it. I reached into my pocket and pulled out a twenty-dollar bill.

"Today I want to answer any questions you may have, but first I want to give you all a pop quiz. The Declaration of Independence is one of our most important documents. In the second paragraph of the Declaration, there are thirty-five words that define the central idea behind our country. It is a moral idea that explains who we are and what we believe about liberty and where it comes from. I will give the first student who can tell me those thirty-five words twenty dollars. Not only that, I'll make it easier for you by telling you the first eleven words. It begins, "'We hold these truths to be self-evident, that all men are . . .'"

Well, twenty dollars is still twenty dollars in any American high school. A dozen hands shot up in the air—all students confident that they knew the answer or were at least willing to take their chances. But, as I called on them one by one, not one came close to the correct answer. I was about ready to give up when one of the more studious-looking boys raised his hand and in a clear voice said, " . . . are created equal, that they are endowed by their Creator with certain unalienable Rights, that among these are Life, Liberty and the pursuit of Happiness."

"You're absolutely right," I shouted as the proud boy moved forward to collect his twenty dollars, while the other students applauded. "OK, now let's talk about those words. What do they mean? It says we are all created equal and endowed by our Creator—who's that?"

"God," several students shouted.

"Right, and what about unalienable? That means the rights can't be taken away. They are yours as a matter of birthright."

The energy level in the room was now sky-high, and we spent the next half-hour talking about the importance of this idea of God-given rights and how those thirty-five words written so long ago had not only built the foundation for the American republic but had, in fact, changed the world. It was an exciting moment. I wish I could tell you that I had to give up many twenty-dollar bills in the course of the campaign, but unfortunately, in most of the high schools I visited, not one student could give me the correct response. And, significantly, those who came close usually left out the main idea—that our rights come directly from God and thus could not be taken away by government.

What irony and what a tragedy that such a basic fundamental concept about our country is a mystery to many of our kids.

In 1989 many Americans watched in amazement as a spontaneous rebellion erupted at Tiananmen Square in Beijing. Thousands of students gathered to protest against their repressive government. At first the old dictators running Communist China ignored the demonstrators hoping they would fade away. But when liberty is first experienced by enslaved people, it is intoxicating. With each passing hour the crowds grew, and the students were joined by other segments of Chinese society—

disgruntled workers, merchants, mothers, and teachers. Petitions listing grievances were circulated and signed. Papier-mâché models of our Statue of Liberty were built and paraded through the streets. The ruling authorities began to tremble at the possibility that their power was in jeopardy. They ordered the People's Liberation Army (PLA) to disband the crowd.

The students were told to leave or be shot. Witnesses who survived what happened next said that many of the young Chinese students reached into their pockets and pulled out copies of our Declaration of Independence. They waved those words in the faces of the PLA soldiers just before they opened fire. By some estimates, thousands of Chinese were killed or wounded that day by their own government for the crime of embracing the idea of America—that liberty is a birthright from God.

There is not a tyrant in the world, whether he is in Cuba, North Korea, Bosnia, or Iraq who rests easy at night because of the fear that those he oppresses may read and understand this central idea. Chinese students were willing to die for those words, though most of them had never set foot in America. Yet in one high school after another, I found American kids who had no idea that the words even existed.

We live in a time when the messages our children receive define America as a place where you can do whatever you want, and that the purpose of life is to accumulate wealth. Such a society would be empty indeed. Youth, particularly, need to be inspired with a greater purpose than just their own self-interest. John F. Kennedy did it through the Peace Corps and the space

> **We live in a time when the messages our children receive define America as a place where you can do whatever you want, and that the purpose of life is to accumulate wealth. Such a society would be empty indeed.**

program, and tens of thousands of America's youth responded. Ronald Reagan did it by explaining what was at stake in the Cold War and explaining why America is a "shining city on a hill" in a world of dark forces, and he restored in young and old alike a sense of pride in our country and its institutions.

During the campaign I proposed that we could go far toward inspiring our children if we began the school day in American high schools with a reading of the second paragraph of the Declaration of Independence. What a wonderful way to remind all of our children—regardless of color, race, or social standing—what it is that made America a unique experiment in self-government. The words of the Declaration can help us achieve racial reconciliation, and they should be the basis of our foreign policy in the world. The founders purposely did not say all Americans are created equal. They said "all men" because they meant us to be a beacon of hope to everyone. Of course they meant all mankind, including women!

A legislator in New Jersey liked my idea and introduced a bill to require the Declaration's central concept to be read each morning in the Garden State schools. Unfortunately, he was voted down. Many legislators complained that the words sounded too much like a prayer! Unbelievable. Others complained that the founders were hypocrites because slavery was allowed in America during the time the Declaration was written. Yes, slavery was allowed, but its death knell was sounded once America embraced those words. Lincoln went back to them time and time again to frame his argument on why our country could not remain half free and half slave. In 1861 he stood on the steps of Independence Hall to speak of the core idea that has kept America united through our darkest nights. The Declaration, he said, offers the promise that in due time, the weights would be lifted from the shoulders of all men, and that all should have an equal chance. He went on

to say that he had no political
idea that did not come from its
principles. "I would rather be
assassinated on this spot than sur-
render it," he said. And, of course,
he did give his life. George Washington ordered that the Declaration be read to his troops,
believing that it would inspire

> The Declaration has always led us to set another place at the table, to expand the American family, and it can lead us to the right solutions to a host of problems.

them to greater sacrifice. Jefferson listed it on his tombstone as one of
his three greatest accomplishments. The Declaration has always led us
to set another place at the table, to expand the American family, and it
can lead us to the right solutions to a host of problems.

The bizarre sentiments and hostility to the Declaration expressed by
some New Jersey legislators are not some sort of oddity, though I wish
they were. A federal district judge actually ruled in the summer of 2000
that my home state of Kentucky could no longer display the key paragraph of the Declaration in schools and county courthouses. The
Declaration was part of a collection of American historical documents
that included the preamble to the Constitution of Kentucky, which
states, "We, the people of the Commonwealth of Kentucky, grateful to
Almighty God for the civil, political and religious liberties we enjoy, and
invoking the continuance of those blessings, do ordain and establish this
constitution." Also in the historical display were the national motto, "In
God We Trust," the Mayflower Compact, and a letter from Abraham
Lincoln declaring April 30, 1863, a National Day of Prayer and
Humiliation. Fox News commentator Tony Snow suggested the federal
court ruling clearly demonstrates "that even blockheads may become
federal judges." If only our problem was just blockheads! Unfortunately,
too many American elites disdain our country's founding values.

THE DECLARATION ACCORDING TO
PETER WOODBURY SCHOOL

Now for the good news. I began the book by telling you that I felt better about America at the end of my campaign than I did at the beginning, and this issue is no exception. In every school I visited, the kids came alive with excitement after I explained the Declaration and its moral foundation to them. They had questions and comments. They were disappointed when the sessions were over. Their reactions and passion convinced me that we can inspire a new generation of our children with the idea of America.

In the last week of my campaign, I had the proof of that brought home to me in a dramatic way. My family and I and a few key staff people left Iowa late the night of the Iowa caucuses. I had not done as well in the vote as I had hoped, and it was apparent that my campaign was almost over. The New Hampshire primary was only one week away. Many of my own staff urged me to drop out that very night, but it just didn't feel right to me. Instead, we spent most of our two-hour flight talking and praying about whether to continue in the race through the primary or drop out and call it quits. By the time we landed, I had concluded that it would be unfair to our friends in New Hampshire to leave the race before the vote. They had worked hard and taken a risk on my underdog candidacy, and I was not about to abandon them. It was already two o'clock in the morning. We went to our hotel, caught a few hours of sleep, and woke to a beautiful New Hampshire snowstorm. I tried to get my spirits up and headed to our first event at Peter Woodbury School in Bedford, New Hampshire, where the fifth-grade teachers had invited me to meet with their classes. After braving heavy snow and icy roads and arriving at the school about forty-five minutes late, it felt like this could be the beginning of a pretty discouraging day on the campaign trail. But I had no idea what awaited me inside that

44

very special school. Every candidate who has ever wondered if the trials, exhaustion, travel, and separation from your family are worth the effort deserves an experience like the one I was about to enjoy.

We were greeted at the door by four students wearing "Bauer for President" T-shirts. (Don't worry about political bias. Each of the candidates was invited to come to the school, and each one that accepted was greeted by a similar welcoming committee.) The students walked me into a room with over a hundred chairs in a semicircle and one seat in the middle—for me.

The teachers, Diane Zito and Virginia Toland, told me they had read in the newspaper that I had been disappointed by how few American high-school students knew the second paragraph of the Declaration of Independence. They asked me to just sit back and relax because they had a surprise for me. One of the teachers nodded to one little girl who quickly jumped to her feet and said, "Mr. Bauer, When in the course of human events it becomes . . ." And she sat down. A boy stood and picked up the sentence from there. As I sat there astonished, those kids recited not just the second paragraph, but the entire Declaration of Independence from memory. They did it with enthusiasm and energy. They did it like they knew what the words meant. The Founding Fathers would have been proud!

I immediately fell in love with each of these children and the teachers who had so lovingly passed on to them one of the most important things they will ever be taught—that liberty is a gift from God and must be tempered with virtue.

> **I immediately fell in love with each of these children and the teachers who had so lovingly passed on to them one of the most important things they will ever be taught—that liberty is a gift from God and must be tempered with virtue.**

I thought about all the teachers in my own life who had inspired me to see beyond the limits of the rough streets I grew up on, who first made our nation's incredible history come alive for me. A good teacher can change your life forever, and these kids had good teachers!

After a bruising campaign, then drawing to a close, those kids at Peter Woodbury School were food for my soul. They reminded me again of the potential of our country, a potential that is reborn with the birth of each American child. These children were not yet infected with the pervasive cynicism of our age. They were not being taught to despise their country, but to love it and to work to make it better. By air, Bedford, New Hampshire is not far from the scandals and power struggles of Washington, D.C. But that morning, Washington, with its constant battles over the getting and the keeping of power, seemed a million miles away.

After their dramatic rendition of the Declaration, the children had one more surprise. They had composed a song that explained something central about every American president. They sang it to the tune of "Yankee Doodle Dandy." I want to share it with you. Maybe it will help interest your child or grandchild in our history.

FDR and JFK, Reagan, Johnson, Lincoln
Ran our country very well by using their persuasion.

Bush and Adams and Monroe, Coolidge, Taft, and Hoover,
These presidents worked very hard; they were our country's movers.

Buchanan, Clinton, Cleveland, Johnson, they were all reformers.
They made changes to our country, reaching all four corners.

Wilson, Harding, Madison, Nixon, Polk, and Carter,
They all had intelligence which made them even smarter.

Jackson, Taylor, Roosevelt, William Henry Harrison, and
Truman they were all tough men when they ran our nation.

Martin Van Buren, Gerry Ford, John Tyler, Rutherford B. Hayes
At the right time they were all just sitting in the right place.

J. Q. Adams and McKinley, Arthur, Pierce, and Fillmore,
They all had experience that helped us run our land more.

Leadership, experience, and working hard are all fine.
Jefferson, he had them, for he was one of a kind.
Being well rounded is the best, it proves effective,
Just like Thomas Jefferson, it helps to be eclectic!

And that wasn't all. They sang one more verse about what the Bauer presidency would be dedicated to.

Gary Bauer's a candidate who hopes to lead our nation
As the moral conservative, he uses his persuasion
So all local communities can control education
Defending family, faith, and freedom is his dedication.

I couldn't have said it better myself. I probably should have hired them to handle public relations in my campaign!

I found out later that many of the students at Peter Woodbury cried when they watched a tape of me dropping out of the race that Tuesday night after the vote. One of the fifth graders told her teacher, "He really likes us! He cared about what we thought!" Well, I loved, not just liked, those kids. Along with all of our children, they are sitting on the shoulders of giants—men and women who were willing to pay any price and make any sacrifice to build this great country. We owe it to these children to not just prepare them for the jobs of the future, but also to give them an appreciation of the past. We owe it to them so that the cynicism of our age doesn't overwhelm their stout hearts and loving spirits. It is one of the main reasons that I ran for president. To the students at Peter Woodbury and every other school I visited: Don't ever give up on our country. We are counting on each of you to dream great dreams, reach for the stars, and make America all it can be.

CHAPTER 4

—◦∞◦—

BABY HOPE

When I decided in early 1999 to throw my hat in the ring for the GOP presidential nomination, I had a fundamental question to answer—what kind of candidate would I be? Would I run a symbolic campaign in an effort to influence the debate on a particular issue? Or would I offer a governing vision that would demonstrate to voters I had ideas on the full range of issues facing the American people. It wasn't that hard of a call for me. I wanted the nomination and I intended to run a real, not symbolic, candidacy.

Over the next six months, I outlined a broad agenda. On the issue of taxes, I gave a major speech at the National Press Club calling for a fair flat tax that provided recognition for the fact that much of our nation's wealth is made up of human capital, not just things. On foreign policy, I outlined a Reaganesque vision in major speeches delivered at Harvard and the prestigious Commonwealth Club in San Francisco. I issued policy papers on trade, agriculture, and the environment. I put on the table my own Social Security reform proposal, which would preserve the system as a safety net, while giving younger workers a 20 percent payroll tax cut that they could invest anywhere they chose, including in their families and children. As the former number two man in the Department of Education, I put a major emphasis on reforming our schools in a way that would empower parents, guarantee local control, and strengthen curriculum and accountability.

Many of these major speeches and foreign-policy proposals received significant press attention. Combined with the six presidential debates I took part in that covered the spectrum of issues that would face the next occupant of the Oval Office, we were able to convince many political observers that my campaign was not merely a symbolic effort, nor was it a one-issue campaign.

> **The fact is that the life issue must be a fundamental question in American politics. America can and must offer more to women and our children than the option of taking innocent human life.**

In spite of this, some hostile reporters and talking heads on television tried to marginalize my candidacy. They would simply refer to me as the "pro-life candidate," or their phrase of choice, "the antiabortion candidate." No doubt their intention was to scare certain swing voters or to send a signal that my campaign wasn't real. Well, I rejected that analysis by the media elites during my campaign, and I reject it now. The fact is that the life issue must be a fundamental question in American politics. America can and must offer more to women and our children than the option of taking innocent human life.

Just a few weeks before I traveled home to northern Kentucky to announce my candidacy, an incredible incident occurred in Cincinnati, Ohio, just a few miles from my childhood home. A nineteen-year-old woman was seeking a late-term abortion and had completed the first day of the three-day process. The next morning she awoke with severe abdominal pain and was rushed to a suburban Cincinnati hospital where she gave birth to a live baby girl, twenty-two weeks into her pregnancy. The newborn baby, who was supposed to be aborted, instead became the "dreaded complication" for those who perform late-term abortions—a live child.

The nurses and doctors at the hospital that day were trained to preserve life. Under any other circumstances they would have leaped into action to help this premature child breathe and survive. Medical advances now allow us to save many such children. But not this time. The young woman was seeking an abortion, not a birth; an end to this inconvenience, not a baby. The nurses wrapped the child in blankets to make her as comfortable as possible. One nurse named the infant Baby Hope and rocked her for hours until she passed away because of insufficient lung development. The event was so dramatic that the health professionals who witnessed it had to undergo professional counseling.[1]

My heart broke when I learned of Baby Hope's birth and tragically short life. Can it really be that under the Constitution of the United States that innocent little child had no rights? Can it really be true that there is no room in America for her and the other one and a half million children who lose their lives every year in the name of the right to choose? I believe we are a better nation than that, and I think America's unease with abortion on demand is growing as we begin to consider more seriously the humanity of our unborn children.

> Can it really be that under the Constitution of the United States that innocent little child had no rights? Can it really be true that there is no room in America for her ?

THE CULTURE OF *ROE V. WADE*

Our nation never voted for the current abortion law. It was imposed on our country in 1973 when the Supreme Court in *Roe v. Wade* found a "right to privacy" in the Constitution that included a right to abortion. Of course there is no such right mentioned in the Constitution. In fact, just the opposite is true. In the Declaration of Independence, there is a specific right to life, liberty, and the pursuit of happiness that the Court completely ignored.

I believe they made a horrifying mistake in the *Roe* decision that is reminiscent of another mistake the Supreme Court made in the 1850s. In the Dred Scott case, the Court ordered the return of a runaway slave to his owner. The court concluded that slaves, black men and women, had no rights the rest of us were bound to respect. That infamous decision helped to rip the nation asunder in a conflict that turned father against son, neighbor against neighbor, state against state, and almost destroyed the Union. Today, nearly a century and a half later, we continue to be burdened with the poison it unleashed. It keeps us apart and eats at our souls.

Roe was a similar mistake. It took a whole class of Americans, our unborn children, and stripped them of any constitutional protection. Each year new scientific research proves the humanity of the unborn child—their ability to feel pain, a heartbeat eighteen days after conception, brain waves forty days after

> **Roe was a . . . mistake. It took a whole class of Americans, our unborn children, and stripped them of any constitutional protection.**

conception, and now new evidence that the fetus can actually remember. More than one abortionist has ended his practice after seeing an unborn child recoil from his abortion tools. *Roe* has given us a country where Baby Hope is unwelcome, a "complication." Our healthcare professionals don't even know what to do with such a child—save her or let her die? Our law says such a child is on her own.

In four straight presidential debates, my campaign drew by lot the right for me to ask another candidate the first question of the debate. Since Governor Bush was the front runner, I chose each time to pose my question to him. In three of those debates, I pressed him on the issue of life. I did that not to irritate him or his supporters, but because it is a fundamental issue for our country and for the nominee of the party of Lincoln.

Abortion on demand will be ended in America in only one way: A future Supreme Court will overturn *Roe v. Wade*. Since it is likely that there will be several Supreme Court vacancies in the next few years owing to the health and age of the nine justices now serving, I wanted to know how Bush would handle his Court appointments. Would his appointees embrace the fundamental right to life of all of us, who according to our Declaration of Independence are "created equal"? The governor consistently and firmly refused to make such a commitment. Much to my persistent disappointment, he said repeatedly there would be no "litmus tests" on Court appointees. Many hope and believe that his answer was merely political. Under this theory, he was trying to avoid providing ammunition to his political enemies who would use it to undermine him with women voters. Perhaps so, but I found it troubling nonetheless. I can tell you from my eight years at the highest levels of the federal government that there will be incredible resistance, even within a Republican administration, to the appointment of pro-life justices.

Now that President Bush is in office, the signals are even more confusing. Even before he took office, Laura Bush told Katie Couric in a *Today Show* interview that *Roe v. Wade* should not be overturned. And even former Senator and now Attorney General John Ashcroft, who had a strong pro-life record in Congress, caused a few raised eyebrows when he told the Senate Judiciary Committee that *Roe v. Wade* was "settled law." His answer was understandable given the nasty attack he was under at the time. But no court decision that excludes defenseless children from the American family and the protection of the Constitution can ever be "settled." Thankfully, while pro-life marchers conducted their annual March for Life in Washington on January 22, 2001, President Bush repealed a Clinton-era executive order, thus ending the funding by U.S. taxpayers of abortions abroad. But this is only a small first step. Much more must be done to change the law and to educate the public.

The abortion culture is hardening our hearts. The philosophical rationale of *Roe v. Wade* has unleashed an attack on the sanctity and dignity of each human life that should be of grave concern to all Americans. Princeton University has come under heavy criticism for awarding an influential endowed seat at its Center for Human Values to Peter Singer. Singer argues that newborn babies and infants are not real people (the same thing that is said of unborn children) because they are not "rational and self-aware." He has suggested that babies should not be admitted to the "community" as citizens until they are one month old. And of course if they aren't "citizens," they have no rights. He has argued that an infant with a condition as mild as hemophilia can be killed as long as the killing has no "adverse effects on others." In Singer's view, this would enable parents to "replace" the child with one "likely to have a better life." And in case anyone is confused about the implication of all this, he has asserted, "Killing a disabled infant is not morally equivalent to killing a person. Very often it is not wrong at all."

Singer has gone on to argue that it is ethical to "harvest" organs from disabled babies and has raised similar arguments about the elderly. He argues that "the notion that human life is sacred just because it's human life is medieval."[2]

Singer's views are outrageous, but because he has raised them they are "debat-

> A great nation cannot allow such things without undermining its reason for greatness. And we are great because we established at our founding that life is a gift from God, and that with life comes a birthright that cannot be taken away by any government.

able," and as they are debated, they will become acceptable to some people. Already on the floor of the U.S. Senate, there has been debate over how much of a baby's body can be out of the womb in the process of being born and still be legally aborted by the doctor. A great nation cannot allow such things without undermining its reason for greatness. And we are great because we established at our founding that life is a gift from God, and that with life comes a birthright that cannot be taken away by any government.

THE PROOF OF LIFE

My hope, as always, resides with average Americans. Polls show pro-life sentiment steadily growing. Every day on the campaign trail I met women who had chosen abortion and now were fighting on the pro-life side to restore protection to unborn children. But perhaps the most moving story I heard was one in which I played a direct part, unbeknownst to me until the Sunday morning before the Iowa caucuses.

My family and I attended services at First Assembly of God in Des Moines, where the theme that Sunday was the importance of strong families and involved fathers and the impact parents can have on their youngsters. The sermon was movingly presented by Josh McDowell, well-known speaker and author, and as he wove into his talk words about the strong faith of our daughter Sarah, whom he had met the night before, the dad in me swelled with pride. I remember standing there with my family as the huge congregation sang with such feeling. Though we were all exhausted and anxious from the string of long days and short nights, I already knew that whatever the outcome, I had made the right decision in choosing to seek the nomination. Carol later told me that tears welled in her eyes as she watched our family being fed by the message and the music, and that she, too, felt affirmation that morning.

After the service ended, I was swarmed by parishioners who wished me well in the next night's voting. In the midst of all the activity, I looked over and saw Carol deep in serious conversation with a woman from the church. I could tell Carol was emotionally moved by what the woman was telling her. Soon she was being shown a picture, and at one point the two of them hugged. When the crowd had thinned, Carol motioned me over, introduced me, and simply said that this woman had a story to tell me.

The story the woman related has impacted me to this day. Ten years before she found herself in a crisis pregnancy and had decided to have an abortion. On the way to the clinic, she had popped a tape given to her by an acquaintance into her car cassette player. It turned out to be a speech I had given on choosing life over abortion. She pulled off the road, wept, and canceled the appointment to have an abortion. The evening after we met at the church, this woman brought her nine-year-old son with her to meet me at a campaign event. The boy, who knew the story of how close he came to being aborted, cried when he met me and said that in some ways he felt as if I were his father! His mother gave me a picture of them, which I keep as a constant reminder that life is one issue always worth fighting for.

> Anyone who has met [them] would be hard-pressed to make the case that some of these precious children should not have been born.

Others, too, are standing up for life. I was incredibly excited to be endorsed by Kenny and Bobbi McCaughey, the parents of septuplets born in 1997 in Carlisle, Iowa. Bobbi had taken the fertility drug Pergonel after having trouble conceiving their first child, Mikkayla. When ultrasound tests showed that Bobbi was carrying seven unborn children, there were those in the medical profession who felt a "pregnancy reduction" should take place to destroy some of the unborn children, theoretically giving the remaining ones a better chance of survival. Bobbi and Kenny never considered it. They believed that all of the children had been given to them by God.

Anyone who has met Kenneth, Alexis, Natalie Sue, Kelsey Ann, Brandon James, Nathaniel Ray, and Joel Steven, as I have, would be hard-pressed to make the case that some of these precious children should not have been born. Each of them, when they were created, possessed the human dignity and the right to life that all of us have been given.

CHANGING THE HEART

Americans are good and decent people. I believe with moral political leadership they will reject this culture of death. Support for *Roe v. Wade* is steadily dropping. Just weeks after I announced my candidacy, I was heartened by a Gallup/CNN/*USA Today* poll that found that 58 percent of the public either wants abortion to be "illegal in all circumstances" or "legal only in a few circumstances." Even more encouraging is the growing evidence that women, the other victim in every abortion, are rejecting this so-called women's right. Seventy percent of women want more restrictions, and most would allow abortion only in the cases of rape, incest, or to save the mother's life.

The movement by the public in the pro-life direction gives lie to the excuses of politicians who claim that they are against abortion but contend that nothing can be done about it until hearts are changed. The hearts of the American people, on balance, already reject the assault on defenseless children, the

> **If abortion has aided anyone, it has been young men, who polls say are the largest supporters of abortion on demand. It empowers them to abandon the women they have impregnated and exploited.**

aged, sick, and disabled through abortion and euthanasia. Ironically, the same politicians who talk about changing hearts are the very ones who seldom use speeches, debates, or political capital to lead hearts to change.

The across-the-board legalization of abortion and the celebration of it as empowering women and putting them in charge of their reproductive rights has in reality been no such thing. Half the babies aborted are, of course, girls. In fact, the number is larger in some cultures that abort baby girls so that the firstborn can be a son. Women are often deeply damaged by abortion and wracked by guilt for the loss of their unborn child. If abortion has aided anyone, it has been young men, who polls say are the largest supporters of abortion on demand. It empowers them to abandon the women they have impregnated and exploited.

During the darkest days of the Civil War, President Abraham Lincoln was asked how much longer the terrible conflict would continue. His reply was that he feared God would let it go on until enough blood had been shed, North and South, to equal all the blood drawn by the slave master's lash. What would a just God demand of America today for all of the ripped flesh and spilled blood of one and a half million abortions a year?

I believe with all of my heart that America is better than this. I think we must welcome all of our children into the world and protect them under the law. There is a place at the table for each one of them.

> I think we must welcome all of our children into the world and protect them under the law. There is a place at the table for each one of them.

As my campaign entered its final days in New Hampshire, a key state political reporter took me aside. "Gary, you have run an honorable campaign. Your range of expertise on a host of issues surprised a lot of people. If you had not brought up that abortion issue so much, I think you could have surprised people on Election Day here in New Hampshire," he said.

I thanked him but told him it would not have been worth running if I had to abandon the most defenseless Americans to advance my own political ambitions. Ronald Reagan said in his last interview as president that his biggest regret was not having overturned *Roe v. Wade* and returning all of our children to the American family. He knew this issue was bigger than the typical political calculations. In fact in 1980, Reagan would not accept George Bush as his running mate unless Bush changed his views on abortion, which he did.

I will never sacrifice one American child, born or unborn, rich or poor, for political gain. And I will never stop trying to challenge the hearts and minds of Americans on this issue. On this I cannot and will not be moved.

CHAPTER 5

DUTY, HONOR, COUNTRY

General Douglas MacArthur's farewell address to West Point is a rhetorical monument to the millions of Americans who have defended our nation over the course of its 225-year history. In his speech, MacArthur focused on three words: duty, honor, and country. I tried to come back to these words in every speech I made on the campaign trail. What is our duty to each other and to our country? What does honor require of us as free men and women facing the great challenges of the world we live in? Can we recapture these core values and teach them to our children?

I can tell you without hesitation that Americans still care deeply about these values. Most of us still agree with MacArthur that duty, honor, and country "reverently dictate what you ought to be, what you can be, what you will be. They are your rallying point to build courage when courage seems to fail, to regain faith when there seems to be little cause for faith, to create hope when hope becomes forlorn."

MONUMENTS OF COURAGE

From one end of Washington, D.C., to the other, there are monuments built in honor of America's fighting men who for over two hundred years have faithfully answered the call to duty, honor, and country. The one I find most moving is the Vietnam Memorial, designed by Maya Lin to commemorate the fifty-seven thousand Americans killed or missing in that divisive war. It has become the equivalent of an altar, where Americans of all races and backgrounds bring symbolic sacrifices to their lost loved ones. Photos, flowers, letters, and medals are left each day at the base of the memorial to honor those who made the ultimate sacrifice. Many times, when I was not on the campaign trail but in our headquarters outside of Washington, D.C., I would drive in to the memorial to remind myself of what real heroism is. I was only dodging the bullets of editorial writers, talking heads, and political opponents. The men and women whose names are written on the face of the Vietnam Memorial had to confront real bullets on the field of battle. The memorial, as I have written before, has always been for me not only a place of reverence, but a place that helps me put things in perspective.

My father, an old marine, was most moved by the Iwo Jima Memorial. Located on the Virginia side of the Potomac River, it captures in bronze the heroic raising of the American flag by my dad's fellow leathernecks on that South Pacific island during

> But things were different then. There was a consensus in our country that the future depended on God's hand of protection.

World War II. Six men are depicted in the sculpture, but there are thirteen hands on the flagpole—the extra hand meant to symbolize God's presence in the middle of that horrific battle. Today it probably couldn't be built on public property without the ACLU and other lawsuit-happy special-interest groups challenging its religious imagery. But things were different then. There was a consensus in our country that the future depended on God's hand of protection. In fact, FDR didn't hesitate to lead the nation in prayer over the radio during the darkest days of World War II.

Incredibly, the Iwo Jima Memorial is the only currently completed Washington, D.C., monument erected in honor of "the greatest generation," who defeated Hitler and his storm troopers and prevented the world from descending into a long nightmare of despair. Fortunately, a World War II memorial is planned for the Washington Mall. It will sit in that great expanse of land between the Washington Monument at one end and the Lincoln Memorial at the other. And the little community of Bedford, Virginia, that suffered the largest per capita number of casualties on D-day, has constructed what they hope will become a national D-day monument. Bedford lost twenty-one of its men that day in 1944, out of a population of only 3,400. It was the home of Company A of the 116th Infantry. Of the thirty-five Bedford soldiers, nineteen died within the first fifteen minutes of the invasion, and two more died later that day.

When Dwight David Eisenhower reviewed the reports of bravery on the beaches of Normandy, he asked rhetorically, "Where do we get such men?" Of course, he already knew the answer to his question. We got them where we always have—from every little town and big city, every suburb and farm, every field and factory, from one coast to the other, where Americans have been raised to love their country and taught that liberty does not come cheaply. Sixteen million Americans served in uniform during World War II, and four hundred thousand of them died in the fighting.

How appropriate that the World War II generation would come home from Europe and the South Pacific and just go about their business. They did not clamor for honors nor lobby for acclaim. My mother lost two of her brothers during World War II and took care of my father's grandfather while he was in the South Pacific. She was just a kid herself, but the times made people grow up fast. The World War II era consists of a million stories like this of incredible individual sacrifice by average Americans. But through it all they just did their jobs, survived the nightmare, and came home hoping to start their families and get on with their lives.

On a recent trip home, my mother and I sat in the living room where I grew up and talked about those years. She went to the closet and pulled out a small suitcase, set it on the couch between us, and carefully opened it. The musty smell of age and old paper floated out. Inside were my mother and father's mementos of the heart, the remembrances like those that sit in boxes in

> **My dear Mrs. Bauer:**
> **I regret to inform you of the report just received that your husband, Private First Class Stanley R. Bauer, U.S. Marine Corps Reserve, sustained a shrapnel wound of the shoulder in action against the enemy on 29 September 1944 in the Palau Islands.**

the attics and basements of millions of American homes. My father's purple hearts—he was wounded in action twice—were in a small plastic bag. In one corner was a stack of postcards and letters he sent from different ports, along with a small black book where he had meticulously written the name of each new place he was sent by the marines. The list reads like a roll call of the killing fields in the South Pacific.

In one envelope were two letters that had been carefully folded and saved. Written six months apart and sent from Headquarters U.S. Marine Corps, they informed my mother of the wounds suffered by Dad in combat.

One dated December 16, 1944, read,

My dear Mrs. Bauer:

I regret to inform you of the report just received that your husband, Private First Class Stanley R. Bauer, U.S. Marine Corps Reserve, sustained a shrapnel wound of the shoulder in action against the enemy on 29 September 1944 in the Palau Islands.

Because of the great volume of communications now required for essential military operations, the report was necessarily brief and did not disclose the extent of his injuries. . . .

Your anxiety is realized and any additional information received will be promptly furnished to you.

Imagine what it must have been like to receive such a letter as a young woman with all the responsibilities she had, and not know how badly your husband was wounded, whether he would survive, and what the future would hold. Countless families received such letters that announced a loved one had died on the field of battle or was missing, but they struggled on. My father recovered from his wounds, but he suffered health problems related to them for the rest of his life.

PROMISES MADE

During the campaign, I tried to meet with veterans every chance I got. I spent time talking not only to the World War II vets, whom we are losing at the incredible rate of thirty thousand a month, but also to vets who served in every conflict where the U.S. has defended liberty— Vietnam, Korea, Desert Storm, Bosnia. I also visited VA hospitals, where so many veterans deal with the medical problems that arose from the years of their service.

With no national draft today, there is great risk that these sacrifices made by a few for the sake of many will be underappreciated or taken for granted. It is important that we keep our promises to the men and women who put themselves in harm's way for the rest of us. Of all the places in the federal budget where savings are possible, veteran benefits shouldn't be on the list!

My father spent the last years of his life in the VA hospital in Fort Thomas, Kentucky. Fortunately for him and my mother, it was just a few miles from their home in Newport. My mother visited him virtually every day, rain or shine, sleet and snow, and stayed with him for hours unless she was sidelined with an illness herself. Dad had a leg amputated in his later years. He also suffered from grand mal seizures, which made it impossible for Mom to take care of him. My parents couldn't bring themselves to come live with us in Washington when I served in the Reagan administration, nor during the years that followed. They loved Kentucky and that house they had lived in since I was in the second grade.

> A clear promise was made to his generation and to those that followed: Take care of your country in this time of crisis, and we will take care of you when you come home bearing the wounds of battle.

Dad took great pride in the fact that as a veteran he was entitled to VA health services, as well he should. VA medical services are not welfare. A clear promise was made to his generation and to those that followed: Take care of your country in this time of crisis, and we will take care of you when you come home bearing the wounds of battle. It is a promise we must keep because a great nation keeps its promises. It was signed in blood at places like Pork Chop Hill, the beaches of Normandy, Khe Sanh, Danang, and Somalia. To break it would violate our duty. It would sacrifice our honor. It would bring shame to our country.

But arguably, we are breaking that promise. All over the country during my presidential campaign, I saw evidence of declining services for our veterans. Many hospitals and treatment centers are being closed and consolidated with other facilities as a cost-cutting measure. These are the bloodless judgments of number-crunchers looking at balance sheets. But no balance sheet in Washington can accurately reflect the real flesh and blood that is involved. Consolidated facilities mean that many veterans can only find medical and rehabilitation services miles and miles from home. Loved ones are unable to visit regularly because of the distances that have to be traveled. My mother's daily visits were great medicine for Dad, and they were good for her too. They had been married for forty years! But in many parts of the country today, so many facilities have been closed that families aren't able to do what my mother did. Consolidation in New Hampshire has meant that families have to drive to Boston to visit their loved ones. Cost cutting means VA personnel are overworked and pressed to the limits of their physical and psychological capabilities.

I have seen an attitude among Washington bureaucrats, and even at the highest levels of the Pentagon, that is disturbing. During Desert Storm thousands of men and women in the reserves were called up along with regular full-time active-duty units. The U.S. demonstrated incredible technological superiority in the air during the conflict, but like all wars, troops had to be on the ground in a hostile environment in order to secure victory. There were deep concerns about the possibility that Saddam Hussein would use biological or chemical warfare. U.S. soldiers were given a variety of vaccines and shots to guard against the possibility. In addition, our forces were exposed to incredible environmental hazards when Hussein torched oil wells, which burned out of control for days.

When U.S. soldiers returned home, many began to experience serious health problems. Previously healthy men and women were suddenly chronically ill. They experienced symptoms consistent with compromised immune systems—skin lesions, loss of hair, digestive problems, and a host of other problems—eventually labeled Gulf War Syndrome.

What was the attitude in Washington? There was official resistance to conceding that the medical problems were related to military duty. There were veiled suggestions that the soldiers were goldbricking.

Others in government suggested that Gulf War veterans were trying to get benefits for psychosomatic illness, or worse, for no real illness at all. There were calls for one study after another while real people with real families suffered. And since the research could not find one single explanation for the symptoms the veterans experienced, the official attitude has been to deny the suffering.

When these same men and women were doing their job in Desert Storm, no one questioned their character. When National Guard and reserve units left jobs, careers, and families, they were held up for acclaim—as they should have been. But now these same soldiers face closed doors and indifferent politicians. How convenient for the number-crunchers in the Washington bureaucracy.

I met many of these veterans on the campaign trail. More than once I looked into their eyes and at their families. I saw men and women who were sick, and they were scared because they didn't know why. I met good Americans who felt abandoned by their country. We have seen this pattern before. Vietnam veterans went through similar bureaucratic resistance as evidence grew that exposure to Agent Orange, a toxic element used in ground combat against the Vietcong, was causing a variety of serious illnesses.

Enough is enough. Obviously, veterans' benefits and medical care are paid for with American tax dollars. There should be due diligence to make sure that money is neither wasted nor paid out inappropriately. Having said that, we must stop acting like Scrooge when it comes to honoring our promises to the men and women who have risked so much for the rest of us.

PROMISES TO KEEP

I spoke with men and women currently on active duty from air bases like Elmendorf to the naval yards in Virginia Beach. Today's armed forces serve during a time in which no war has been declared, but ironically, they are almost always on the front lines. Many of the sailors who perished on the USS *Cole* were eating lunch when a terrorist bomb delivered in a small suicide boat blasted a forty-foot hole in the side of their ship. My

These events serve as a vivid reminder that while we enjoy lives of relative security, safe in our homes and our jobs, other Americans are in harm's way, standing watch on the tower. They do so at a great cost to their families and loved ones.

blood boiled when the *Washington Post* reported that sailors on sentry duty aboard the *Cole* carried unloaded guns and weren't authorized to shoot unless fired upon. One petty officer, "with blood still on my face," reported that even after the terrible attack, when a second small boat approached, he was ordered to turn his gun away.[1] These are the types of rules made by Washington bureaucrats, secure in their offices while others patrol unfriendly seas. The devastating attack on the marine barracks in Beirut, Lebanon, took place when the men were asleep. These events serve as a vivid reminder that while we enjoy lives of relative security, safe in our homes and our jobs, other Americans are in harm's way, standing watch on the tower. They do so at a great cost to their families and loved ones. And as always, some are called to pay the ultimate price, to which the fresh crosses and Stars of David in our nation's cemeteries attest.

We have an obligation to these men and women too, and in recent years it has not been met. Morale among active-duty troops has been at rock bottom in recent years. At Elmendorf, I met a young pilot who reflected this frustration. He had a job to do, but increasingly, he didn't have the tools to do it. A number of aircraft in his squadron were grounded because parts had been cannibalized from them to

keep other jets in the air.
Foreign commitments during
the '90s were increased, while
the number of men and
women in uniform declined
and resources shrank. There
has been a major increase in

> **Shame on us. Shame on our political leadership that shortchanges the greatest armed forces the world has ever seen.**

deployments away from home, and they last for longer periods of time.

Compensation has also continued to lag, and as a result, military families are experiencing unprecedented strains and family breakup is at a record high. Because of the low rate of pay, eight thousand army personnel are on food stamps. This in a country enjoying the largest economic boom in our history. In Washington, D.C., and surrounding communities, I know of young military families who drive around at the crack of dawn on the weekends to look for furniture left at the curbside as trash by their more-well-off neighbors.

Shame on us. Shame on our political leadership that shortchanges the greatest armed forces the world has ever seen. The decline of readiness in our military forces because of budget cuts became a campaign issue last November, and I would like to think that my repeated emphasis on the issue played some role in that.

In the years ahead it is imperative that our military have the equipment and the resources they need. In addition, the commander in chief, of whatever party, must be an individual whom our soldiers, sailors, and airmen can respect. For eight years we had a president who admitted to conduct that would have ended the career of any U.S. officer. Hopefully, those days are over for good.

The incredible movie *Saving Private Ryan* ends with a poignant scene. Private Ryan morphs from a young soldier to a man in his twilight years, standing before the cross at Normandy that marks the grave of the man who died rescuing him. He thanks him for all the years he was given as a result of that heroic sacrifice.

We have been rescued too. Time and time again our liberty has been safeguarded by brave and selfless men and women. The American military has always been freedom's army—not an army of conquest, nor an army of territorial expansion. Twice America's armed forces led the free nations of the world to defeat the great threats of the century. We fought against Soviet Communism during the Cold War. Time and again we have liberated, saved, and comforted the weak and defenseless against tyranny. And each time, when the conflict was over, we magnanimously rebuilt our enemies and encouraged them to adopt free institutions.

Not all of us can visit the dramatic vistas of the cemeteries of Normandy. But in your hometown, too, there are places of rest for America's veterans. Take your children there on the special days that mark the journey of freedom. Tell them about what Lincoln called the mystic chords of memory that tie together patriot graves everywhere. Leave a rose or a note of thanks, and in so doing educate the next generation about freedom's wage. You will help them understand that they are sitting on the shoulders of heroes and heroines—that they are truly freedom's children.

And read to them MacArthur's speech on duty, honor, and country in the hope that these noble words will teach them

to be proud and unbending in honest failure, but humble and gentle in success; not to substitute words for actions, not to seek the path of comfort, but to face the stress and spur of difficulty and challenge; to learn to stand up in the storm, but to have compassion on those who fall; to master yourself before you seek to master others; to have a heart that is clean, a goal that is high; to learn to laugh, yet never forget how to weep; to reach into the future, yet never neglect the past;

to be serious, yet never to take yourself too seriously; to be modest so that you will remember the simplicity of true greatness, the open mind of true wisdom, the meekness of true strength.

I made a silent promise at my dad's grave that I would do whatever I could to instill in the rising generation a love for America and an appreciation of the sacrifices made for it. Those who made the sacrifices deserve nothing less.

CHAPTER 6

RELIGIOUS PERSECUTION

For several years I have aggressively spoken out for human rights and political reform around the world. While we cannot and should not militarily intervene every place human rights are being violated, we can speak the truth. And we can use other weapons in our arsenal, including withholding foreign aid from oppressive regimes and, when appropriate, prohibiting access to our marketplace.

Should human rights and related issues impact our trade policy? I think they should, particularly when there are also national security questions that threaten America's safety. For years I have argued that our rush to increase trade with China has been at the expense of our national security and our historic concern about oppression. This debate over Chinese trade has resulted in the formation of two odd coalitions in American politics.

On one side, the alliance consisted of Bill Clinton, Al Gore, the Communist leadership of China, big business groups like the U.S. Chamber of Commerce, the major newspapers, and the GOP leadership in Congress. On the other side, the side I embraced, were veterans' groups like the American Legion and the VFW, human rights activists, the AFL-CIO, Hollywood stars, conservative and liberal members of Congress, and some noteworthy profamily groups like Focus on the Family and the American Family Association.

These unusual alliances resulted in some amazing confrontations. A year or so before I decided to run for president, I was invited by William F.

Buckley Jr., the conservative intellectual and founder of *National Review* magazine, to debate this issue at Ole Miss University before a live audience of six thousand people, with simultaneous coverage on PBS. The team I led included the liberal former governor of California Jerry Brown (now something of a political gadfly), staunchly conservative Senator Tim Hutchinson of Arkansas, and eclectic columnist Arianna Huffington. And our opponents? The team Buckley selected included former Secretary of State Henry Kissinger; James L. Barksdale, the president of high-tech giant Netscape; and Senator Trent Lott of Mississippi, the Republican leader of the Senate.

No wonder many Americans were confused. The China issue had taken the usual alliances in American politics and turned them upside down! As the teams assembled onstage before the debate, the shifting sand of American politics was in stark evidence. Buckley's book *God and Man at Yale* had challenged me and helped form my conservative philosophy when I read it in high school. I admired Barksdale's entrepreneurial achievements. Trent Lott was fighting the good fight on a number of issues in the Senate and is also a longtime friend. But that night they were the opposing team, and on this issue they were wrong.

> **I believe the evidence grows stronger every day that trade with China is changing America much more than it is changing China.**

I don't want to demonize my opponents. That happens far too often in our public life. After all, many of those on the other side are friends and allies on other issues. They truly believe that increased trade with China, or "engagement" as they call it, will change China and slowly make democracy inevitable. But it isn't just political allies that are divided. There are splits in religious ranks too. Some Christian leaders fear that any opposition to Beijing will result in more persecution of missionaries in China. Others don't want to be at odds with the "economic" wing of the GOP. The Christian Coalition went from including the vote against China trade as one of its ranking votes by which to judge members of Congress to a position of neutrality. Pat Robertson wrote a piece for the *Wall Street Journal* parroting the pro-China trade line and attacking me for opposing it. And corporations argue that workers in China will be better off working for divisions of U.S. companies, who are more likely to treat them well.

Sorry, I don't buy it.

I believe the evidence grows stronger every day that trade with China is changing America much more than it is changing China. It has led some business leaders and members of Congress who should know better to avert their gaze from the mounting evidence that oppression is worsening in China. Religious persecution is worsening, not improving. Only the "official" churches are allowed to operate "freely," but to do so they must accept restrictions that violate the conscience. As a result, many believers worship in secret, reading Scripture by candlelight and baptizing their children in the rivers of their country by the dark of night.

Trade with China is creating a "China lobby" in the United States made up of corporate presidents hoping to enrich their bottom lines, politicians afraid to offend these corporations because it would cost them campaign donations, former government officials with lucrative consulting contracts linked to Chinese trade, and current government officials hoping to get such contracts when they leave government service. These individual priorities have overridden all else.

But you don't have to have a soft heart about human rights to be seriously concerned about our China trade policy. Serious analysis would also lead you to conclude that this policy is a failure, simply because it undermines America's national security. Dreams of making great profit in China have prompted American capitalists to sell technology to

China that clearly can be used by its military. The real scandal of the last ten years has not been what China's spies have stolen because of lax security. Shockingly, it has been what we have willingly sold to China in order to fatten the corporate bottom line. During the campaign, I went to some of the corporate headquarters of these companies and held press conferences to bring the light of day to how they were making their profits.

Some of my libertarian friends argue that when people want to do business with one another, government should get out of the way. Sounds good in theory, but in reality many of the companies U.S. firms are doing business with in China are literally owned by the People's Liberation Army (PLA). We aren't doing business with the people of China; we are doing business with their oppressors and, in the process, strengthening the army that our sons and daughters may one day have to face on the battlefield.

There is also no guarantee that if China experiences economic freedom, it will then embrace political freedom and be less of a bad actor on the international stage. History doesn't support that argument. In fact, Nazi Germany experienced an economic recovery under Hitler but lost liberty in the process. And its economic strength was nothing to celebrate. In fact, it made them a more dangerous enemy.

> **We aren't doing business with the people of China; we are doing business with their oppressors and, in the process, strengthening the army that our sons and daughters may one day have to face on the battlefield.**

I am proud of the human-rights alliance of which I have been a part. I believe we are right and that time will prove it. But it was frustrating to hear every major competitor I faced for the presidential nomination on the other side of this fundamental question. Time and again I clashed with Steve Forbes, George Bush, or Orrin Hatch on the issue of China trade. Their arguments made little sense. In an ironic twist, the Bush campaign insisted on writing the China section of the 2000 Republican Party Platform in Austin rather than let the GOP delegates on the Platform Committee draft language that would be firm.

Thankfully, the American people are not as confused on this issue as our political and corporate elites. At the Iowa straw poll in August of 1999, twenty-five thousand people jammed the Hilton Coliseum in Ames to hear Forbes, Bush, Dole, Hatch, Keyes, Alexander, Buchanan, and me outline our platforms. When I said that under my presidency human rights and national security would come first, and that in my first week in office I would repeal most-favored-nation (MFN) status for China, I held my breath for a second waiting for reaction. Iowa farmers desperately need the Chinese market, and it would have been understandable had the audience been ambivalent. Instead, the crowd erupted into the loudest and longest ovation of the day—too loud for the other candidates to ignore. Our farmers want access to foreign markets, including China's, but they are Americans first, and they aren't going to sacrifice their country's interests for their own. By the way, I would restrict technology trade and regulate China's access to our markets unless there was progress on national-security issues and human rights. But I would not use food as a weapon in foreign policy.

STANDING HERE

But enough on policy questions. I want to tell you about some of the men and women I met before and during my campaign who are standing bravely for human dignity and liberty and calling our country to be true to itself and do the same. As always, the heroes and heroines of human rights come in all shapes and sizes.

One of them is a crusading newspaper columnist. I met Abe Rosenthal in 1996 after admiring his columns for many years in the *New York Times*. Abe worked for the *Times* for fifty years, starting as a reporter and ending up as its top editor a few years ago. He "retired" from the editor post and began to write a regular column for the paper he loved and to which he had devoted his life.

Abe has a mighty pen. His sharp words have exposed tyrants from South Africa to Sudan and China. As a Jew, he has particular interest in religious persecution. He understands that when anyone in some dark corner of the world is tortured, imprisoned, or harassed for how they worship God, everyone's faith is under attack. I am sorry to say that Christian leaders have often fallen silent during the persecution of their brothers and sisters in China. Not Abe Rosenthal. He was there time and time again in their defense. We began to call each other regularly to offer mutual encouragement—he a Jew, a liberal, and a Democrat; me a Christian, a conservative, and a Republican!

Media elites are virtually unanimous in supporting trade with China at any cost. Abe's columns were a thorn in the side of the top brass at the *Times*. With virtually no warning, he was called in and told his services were no longer needed. Today, this brave man writes a regular column for Washington's conservative paper, the *Washington Times*. Last year, Abe was honored at a small dinner in New York. His remarks made it clear that he would not call a cease-fire when it comes to human rights. Abe told the audience, "Since Hitler, we Westerners like to say over and over—never again. The gut responsibility for the horrors taking place (in China, Sudan, etc.) will be forever with the rulers of those countries. But those who make them powerful with money and guns in exchange for trade are in my mind equal sinners."[1]

There are heroes and heroines in Congress on this issue too.

One is Representative Nancy Pelosi, Democrat from San Francisco. Nancy and I disagree on virtually everything, but not on this. We worked together against giving China any more trade privileges, and she was willing to take on the president and vice president of her own party. In fact, her indictment of the White House on this matter was tougher than I heard from most Republicans. We held press conferences together on the issue, where Nancy brought liberal groups that were suspicious of me, and I brought conservative groups that worried about her.

On the GOP side of the aisle, the most impressive and consistent voice for human dignity has been Congressman Frank Wolf, who represents a district in northern Virginia outside Washington, D.C. Frank is normally a quiet, unassuming man, but his passions run high when it comes to oppression and the obligation of

> **Nancy and I disagree on virtually everything, but not on this. . . . Her indictment of the White House on this matter was tougher than I heard from most Republicans.**

the United States to never be partner to it. He has put himself on the front lines by traveling to hellholes around the world, where refugees from tyranny are herded into camps or flee into mountains or deserts for safety. He has put himself in harm's way time and time again, staying in refugee camps, feeding the hungry, and comforting the sick. Then he returns to the corridors of power in Washington to speak for those whose voices are drowned out by special interests and the big money that oils the machinery of the nation's capital.

Wolf's first trip to China was in 1991 when he visited Prison No. 11 in Peking, one of the thousands of concrete facilities that make up the Chinese "laigai." His visit came shortly after the Tiananmen Square demonstration, and there were at least forty prisoners whose only crime had been protesting for freedom.

"We're in the middle of the prison—the middle of the prison—and we see that!" Wolf said. "That" was a sign hanging in one of the prison hallways that read, "Beijing Hosiery Factory."[2] Wolf discovered that jelly shoes, then all the craze stateside, and stylish socks were being manufactured with slave labor in the prison for export to fashion-conscious youngsters in the United States. This was no isolated incident—China's prison system doubles as a vast slave-labor network, and its products are aimed squarely at the American consumer market. From Christmas ornaments to running shoes, from jewelry to designer clothes, we Americans subsidize the torture and mistreatment of prisoners of conscience to satisfy our sense of fashion and pocketbook. When will that price be too high?

Another leader on the persecution issue is Nina Shea. Nina is the director of the Center for Religious Freedom at Freedom House. Its January 1996 conference brought one hundred top Christian leaders together to discuss worldwide anti-Christian persecution, and it marked the beginning of church mobilization. Nina grew up a liberal Democrat, but when she published a report on human-rights abuses by the Communists in Nicaragua, her old friends began to shun her. So she started a journey on which she rediscovered her Catholic faith and became a tenacious fighter for the dignity and rights of all of God's children. I am against women in combat, but if I had to be in a foxhole with a lady, I would pick Nina. She is tough, focused, and feminine all at the same time. When the bullets start flying, Nina runs to the front lines, not to the tall grass.

ON THE INSIDE

Even these courageous Americans will tell you their stands on principle pale compared to those in the belly of the beast itself. My biggest worry as I became more vocal on human rights was losing a big donor for the Family Research Council or having the party establishment marginalize me. But for others around the world, their fear is the knock on the door in the middle of the night and the realization that the police or the army or their own country are

My biggest worry as I became more vocal on human rights was losing a big donor for the Family Research Council or having the party establishment marginalize me. But for others around the world, their fear is the knock on the door in the middle of the night.

the enemy. Like our own Founding Fathers, they nonetheless are willing to die for liberty.

In Sudan, Christians and other non-Muslims face what can only be described as genocide at the hands of a radical Islamic regime. The policies of the Sudanese government, including forced starvation and a scorched-earth policy, have resulted in the death of two million people and the displacement of five million more.

The horror is almost unspeakable. Christian women and children in Sudan are sold into slavery, entire villages are destroyed, and the people are herded into Sudanese concentration camps called "peace villages." Christian leaders have been assaulted, tortured, and in some cases, even crucified.

I have helped fight for a trade embargo of Sudan, but the battle has been unbelievably difficult. The country has untapped oil reserves that many would like to exploit. In addition, it exports a soft-drink and fruit-juice additive called gum arabic, which prevents the contents from separating in the can. Our efforts to punish the Sudanese government have been repeatedly derailed by the soft-drink and grocery-store industry, whose lobbyists have twisted arms on Capitol Hill. The embargo now in place is riddled with loopholes that render it ineffective. You would think that shaking our fruit-juice cans would be the least we could do to support freedom.

Even worse, Chinese companies who want to develop Sudan's oil have been permitted to raise capital on Wall Street through public offerings of their stock, all in the name of globalism, commerce, and trade. How many American investors realize they are subsidizing this brutal regime?

One of the most powerful voices against the genocide in Sudan has been Bishop Macram Gassis. He has been forced to live in exile in Nairobi, Kenya, but time and time again he has risked his life by flying into remote areas of Sudan with cargoes of food, building materials, and tools for the people suffering there. This in spite of the fact that if he is captured, he faces arrest and possible crucifixion himself. I met with Bishop Gassis during his trips to Washington and throughout my campaign. I reminded audiences of the horror that was taking place in his country. It is shameful that more isn't being done to save this African Christian. Black leaders like Jesse Jackson who were quick to lead the charge on oppression in South Africa are mute on this issue. African-American churches are just beginning to awaken to this issue. We went to war over the atrocities in Bosnia, but these black human beings don't seem to seize our consciences as much.

I met Gao Xiao Duan when we both testified before the House of Representative's Human Rights Subcommittee on China's one-child policy. For fifteen years, Duan was employed at the Planned Birth Office in Fujan Province. Her job was to help implement the population-control policies of the central government in twenty-two villages, with a population of over sixty thousand. This slight, timid-looking woman found herself a cog in the unbelievable machinery of oppression.

Women in China who violate the one-child policy are subjected to unspeakable horrors, including forced abortions and sterilization. In some cases, violators have their homes literally dismantled piece by piece. Relatives are arrested and imprisoned until women with an unauthorized pregnancy agreed to turn themselves over to authorities.

> **Duan was living in hell. She helped track down neighbors during the day, but at night she had to confront the horror of which she was a part. . . . While helping to implement the government's policy, Duan was in violation of it herself.**

Duan was living in hell. She helped track down neighbors during the day, but at night she had to confront the horror of which she was a part. She told the congressional panel that "my conscience was always gnawing at my heart." In fact, while helping to implement the government's policy Duan, was in violation of it herself.

"We both love children very much," she testified. "Unfortunately, pressed by the one-child policy in Communist China, we could not have a second child. The only thing we could do was to adopt a boy late in 1993. . . . This, however, was in violation of the policy. We had no choice but to keep him in someone else's home we knew through private ties. For fear of being informed against by others in our town, he never called me Mama in the presence of outsiders. When government agencies conducted door-to-door checks, our son had to hide elsewhere. Most of the time he had to stay in our friend's home."

Imagine your own child not being able to acknowledge that you are his mother!

Duan finally reached the breaking point. No matter what her government told her about national policy, she knew she was an accomplice to an evil policy. Few can live a lie for very long and continue to

> **I couldn't help but wonder if those members sitting before this brave young woman were haunted by the parallels to the horrific procedure they had willingly endorsed.**

do things that violate their conscience. Duan told us about seeing a woman nine months pregnant forced to abort her baby after the local communist operatives tracked her down.

"In the operation room, I saw how the aborted child's lips were sucking, how its limbs were stretching." The "doctor" injected poison into the infant's skull, and when the baby died, it was thrown into the trash can. A tearful Duan told the shocked members of Congress, "To help tyrants do evil was not what I wanted, . . . I too, after all, am a mother."[3]

I couldn't help but notice that some of the members of Congress who seemed most upset by the testimony were also the ones who had voted to continue to allow the practice of partial-birth abortion in the United States. These abortions also take place late in the pregnancy. Of course, in the United States, no woman is legally forced to have such an abortion; but the person the procedure matters to the most, the unborn child, has no say at all. I couldn't help but wonder if those members sitting before this brave young woman were haunted by the parallels to the horrific procedure they had willingly endorsed.

Duan closed her testimony with the self-indictment of her actions and a plea to our country. "All of those fourteen years, I was a monster in the daytime, injuring others by the Chinese Communist authorities' barbaric planned-birth policy, but in the evening, I was like all other women and mothers, enjoying my life with my children. I could not live such a dual life anymore. Here, to all those injured women, to all those children who were killed, I want to repent and say sincerely that I'm sorry! I want to be a real human being."[4]

Another witness, Zhou Shau Yon, was pregnant when she fled to the United States, in fear of her own government. She lost her baby in a boat on the way here as she desperately tried to reach freedom. She told Congress how she and other expectant mothers would hide at night in their villages so that the local "female planning" officials wouldn't track them down. Unfortunately, while Yon testified, her own status in America was very much in doubt, and she was facing the possibility of deportation.[5]

Most Americans have never heard of these two women and don't know their stories of resistance to tyranny. But we have seen others through the years who have reminded us of the universal yearning for freedom. I mentioned earlier how disturbing it was to run into students in our high schools who didn't know the central idea of our Declaration of Independence. Yet students in Tiananmen Square held up copies of our Declaration of Independence before they were shot. I remember another image from Tiananmen Square that many of us watched, mesmerized—pictures of a single man standing in front of a People's Liberation Army tank. The tank advanced, but the man would not move. The tank driver blinked first and swerved his tank to the right, but before we could breathe a sigh of relief, the lone protester jumped to the right too, putting himself back in harm's way. No matter which way the soldier in the tank moved, he could not escape that solitary figure who by his very presence was an indictment of tyranny. In that one stark image, the world saw iron and steel and an army of oppression confronting flesh and blood and a heart yearning for liberty.

On June 3, 1999, right in the middle of the battle for the GOP nomination, I spoke at Harvard University to an audience that included survivors of Tiananmen Square. I told them if a democratic future for China becomes a reality, it will be in no small part thanks to the courage and vision of those young Chinese, including the man in front of the tank whose brave witness in 1989 inspired me and millions of others around the world. It doesn't seem like that hard of a choice for me. Either we are on the side of the tank driver or we are on the side of the freedom fighter blocking his path.

WEI JINGSHENG

Finally, I want to tell you about Wei Jingsheng, probably China's best-known dissident. But it wasn't always so. Wei was the son of a pair of mid-level Communist Party officials. As a young man, he believed fervently in Communism. He had been a member of the Red Guard, one of Mao Zedong's most loyal followers during the so-called Cultural Revolution. In that capacity, he began to see the oppression and inequalities of Communism firsthand. In his autobiography, he describes being shocked to see young Chinese children at a train station in rags, filthy, hungry, and begging for food. The other passengers refused to help the children, instead chastising them as "class enemies" of the people. Then, when Wei gave the children his food, others were moved to do so too.[6]

Later, Wei became an electrician at the Beijing Zoo, but the die had been cast. He became known publicly in China when he joined intellectuals who posted essays calling for democracy on a wall in Beijing near the Communist leadership's main compound. For his activities, he was sentenced in October 1979 to fifteen years in jail.

Wei was released for six months and immediately began to speak out again for political and religious freedom in China. In 1994, he met with the U.S. Secretary of State for Human Rights John Shattuck and briefed him on the continuing persecution in China. This infuriated the Chinese government. The Communists arrested him and held him incommunicado for over a year, then subjected him to a show trial, a favorite tactic of dictatorships throughout the last century. In December 1995, he was sentenced to another fourteen years for "engaging in activities in an attempt to overthrow the government." Of course, the charges were a sham and so was the trial. Wei became an international celebrity as political and religious leaders and the news media called for his release. For most of the ensuing two years, I repeatedly lobbied on his behalf, urging the Congress to not reward

> **It proved once again that even the most totalitarian government will respond to world opinion if it thinks there are economic and political consequences.**

the Chinese government in any way as long as political prisoners like Wei were rotting in jail. In November of 1997, Wei was unexpectedly taken from his jail cell, given a few hours with his family, then kicked out of China by the Communist authorities. The news was electrifying for those of us who had pressured China. It proved once again that even the most totalitarian government will respond to world opinion if it thinks there are economic and political consequences.

Wei, supported by those who are working for a free China, has become a powerful voice in America arguing for a China policy that reflects our values. He spent little time recovering from his ordeal in the Chinese prisons and instead came to Washington as quickly as he could. I met him personally for the first time at the home of Ethel Kennedy, the widow of Robert F. Kennedy. In 1994, Wei had been awarded the Robert F. Kennedy Human Rights Award. Mrs. Kennedy, aware of my frequent speeches on Wei's behalf, was kind enough to invite me along with thirty or so of Wei's friends to welcome him to the U.S.

Looking back, I wonder what it must have felt like for Wei, now a free man, to be sitting in the beautiful den of Mrs. Kennedy's home in McLean, Virginia, just days after he huddled on the wet, cold floor of a Chinese prison. A surreal experience, to be sure. Though humbled by the circumstances, Wei chose to use the opportunity to make a prophetic

> Looking back, I wonder what it must have felt like for Wei, now a free man, to be sitting in the beautiful den of Mrs. Kennedy's home in McLean, Virginia, just days after he huddled on the wet, cold floor of a Chinese prison.

prediction. Through an interpreter, he told us that he could safely predict that any former U.S. government official who invested in China would become rich regardless of whether their investment was good or bad. The Chinese Communist government would see to that. They know that the more money Washington's elite make in China, the more likely the elite will be to lobby for a soft policy toward Beijing. He also told us that in the previous years when the Congress had voted for most-favored-nation status for China, the prison guards would use the news to try to break the will of the political prisoners in China.

"See," they would taunt, "even America will not stand with you."

I shuddered as I listened to the price this man had been willing to pay for the freedoms so many in the U.S. take lightly.

I took Wei with me to meet with members of Congress who were undecided on the issue of trade with China. His arguments were powerful and moving and, most importantly, based on firsthand experience. This modern-day freedom fighter could have a profound impact on the issue, I thought. Yet time and time again, good members of Congress turned away and voted with the big corporate lobbyists. Amazingly, only a handful of members even asked to get the CIA briefing on China's military buildup and its potential threat to our national security. One member told Congressman Frank Wolf he didn't want to avail himself of the briefing because his mind was made up to vote "yes" on the trade issue, and he didn't want to see information that would make the vote tougher . . . on him.

Wei should be considered a national resource. He knows China and its leaders better than most of the Washington and business "experts" who are looking at China through rose-colored glasses and seeing nothing but the green of big profits. I am proud that he is my friend and hope in my lifetime to see him back in his homeland—a free China that respects human rights, stops threatening its neighbors, and is a place worthy of our investment.

Meanwhile, we must wake up to the major national-security threat China poses as it thinks about forcible reunification with our ally Taiwan and its 22 million people. After ten years of trade deals with China, it was reported last fall that Chinese officials and military leaders are now openly discussing the inevitability of war with the U.S. Strategists writing in the pages of *China Military Science*, the preeminent Chinese military publication, are publicly considering the possibility of war. One PLA officer wrote, "War is not far from us now." Shen Dingli, a prominent arms-control expert in Shanghai, told the *Washington Post*, "We've never said it so bluntly before. . . . I think China is more clearly preparing for a major clash with the United States."[7]

There doesn't have to be another Asian war involving the United States. But to avoid it we must quit deceiving ourselves about the nature and goals of China's leadership. I spoke up repeatedly during the campaign on this issue, and I promise to continue speaking the truth in the years ahead; not only on behalf of those denied their basic human rights, but also on behalf of the national security and safety of the American people.

CHAPTER 7

—◦∞◦—

HOSTILITY
TO FAITH

On a cold December day in Des Moines, Iowa, all of us still in the race for the GOP nomination gathered for yet another presidential debate. My family and I walked the few blocks to the debate site along streets blocked off to regular vehicular traffic, now lined with satellite television trucks and miles of television cable. Along with a few trusted aides, and in the presence of my strongest supporters, my family and I went through the usual predebate rituals. I tried out a couple of answers on farm issues and China and tried to keep the mood from getting too serious. That would happen soon enough. However, knowing that Iowa voters take their caucus responsibilities very seriously, I was keenly aware that that night was very important.

Mostly though, we all paced around in one of the small holding rooms assigned to each candidate. There were similarities in the setup for the various debates. Usually these rooms were off a common hallway, heavily secured by local police and college-student hosts. Each candidate had their own room for use prior to the event and was also assigned very specific times for makeup and sound and lighting checks. Interestingly, the scheduling of these various steps was so precise that it guaranteed no candidate would inadvertently see another before the big event. My family found this all very amusing. As for me, I thumbed through my briefing book one more time with no idea that the most controversial part of the debate would be something no one could anticipate. Finally, we headed to the auditorium to face another great Iowa audience.

For over an hour each of us verbally sparred on all the usual issues from Medicare reform to gun control and social security. Then, as we entered the home stretch of the debate, moderator Tom Brokaw asked a fascinating question. He wanted to know who was the philosopher or thinker who had the greatest influence on our thinking and philosophy.

Steve Forbes was first in line and said John Locke, a British philosopher whom I doubt few in the audience recognized. Alan Keyes was next and broadly identified the American Founding Fathers. Not much controversy so far. John McCain cited a favorite of mine, Teddy Roosevelt. Roosevelt's fighting spirit, love of country, conservatism, courage, and commitment to fundamental reform have always put him at the top of my list of great U.S. presidents. Senator Orrin Hatch cited Lincoln and Reagan, but it was the answers given by George Bush and myself that caused the most reaction in the days that followed from the talking heads on television and the editorial boards of America's major newspapers. Bush simply said, "Christ, because he changed my heart." The moderator seemed taken aback. "I think the viewers would like to know more on how he's changed your heart," he said. Bush responded, "Well, if they don't know, it's going to be hard to explain. When you turn your heart and your life over to Christ, when you accept Christ as the Savior, it changes your heart. It changes your life. And that's what happened to me."

The Iowa audience, many of whom were religious conservatives, applauded the answer, and I imagined countless more watching on TV did the same. Every day on the campaign trail I met people whose lives had been transformed by their acceptance of Christ as the Son of God. And I had seen the transformation that was possible in my own family. When I accepted Jesus as a young boy in Newport, Kentucky, my alcoholic father walked to the altar with me. We were baptized together. And while he wrestled with alcoholism his entire life, his religious conversion had a transforming effect on his life. Before accepting Christ, my dad saw alcohol as his trusted friend. After accepting Christ, he realized alcohol was his enemy, and he fought it with various degrees of success until his death. I had seen the same impact on drug addicts, criminals, Hollywood stars, millionaires, and even politicians.

I had the last chair on the stage that blustery December evening in Des Moines. There was absolutely no doubt in my mind that, like Bush, Christ was the individual who most impacted my philosophy of life. But I felt the question required more than just a name. It required an explanation. Why should voters

> **What would Christ's influence on my life mean when it came to how I would deal with the poor, the powerless, those hurting or abandoned, or with issues like war and peace?**

care about the answer unless it was relevant to how I would govern as president? What would Christ's influence on my life mean when it came to how I would deal with the poor, the powerless, those hurting or abandoned, or with issues like war and peace?

As the crowd grew quiet, I leaned toward Tom Brokaw and said the first thing that came to mind. "I was hungry and you fed me. I was thirsty and you gave me drink. I was a stranger and you welcomed me. Christ, with those words, taught all of us about our obligations to each other, to the unborn child, to those living in poverty, the need for us to be together regardless of the color of our skin. There is no figure in human history who, through his life, his death, and his resurrection has changed the world for millions . . . of people."

The audience burst into enthusiastic applause, which was gratifying. Our debate moderators, in comparison, looked perplexed. I am not sure that either of them understood that I was quoting the Gospel of Matthew. What we did not know is that at that very moment a tremendous controversy was building around the country, as special-interest groups who want to push religious faith out of the public square reacted to the debate exchange. Press releases were being prepared in New York and Washington by all the usual gatekeepers of respectable opinion to attack the intrusion of religion into American politics.

The *L.A. Times* editorialized, "This sort of pietism leaves Muslims, Jews, Buddhists, Hindus, agnostics, Shamanists and others to see themselves as on the outside."[1] Abe Foxman, national director of the Anti-Defamation League, hurried a letter to us warning that, "Appealing to voters along religious lines is contrary to the American ideal." The *New York Times* and *Washington Post* jumped in too, with similar negative comments, and that weekend every Sunday talk show featured debate on the issue. Even among Christian leaders, my answer and Bush's statement caused chagrin. The Episcopal bishop of Iowa, C. Christopher Epting, got into the fray and assured everyone we were wrong. The good bishop said our mention of Christ was a "turnoff," and he feared "there's going to be heavy-handed Christianity in the White House." In a country with drive-by shootings, widespread promiscuity, fatherless children, a sex-and-violence saturated culture, and nearly eight years of White House scandals, the Christian bishop for Iowa was worried that a future president may make it clear he is a Christian! Columnist Maureen Dowd concluded that Bush's answer and mine were merely political opportunism. She wrote, "This is the era of niche marketing and Jesus is a niche. . . . Christ is polling well in Iowa. Christ is the new wedge issue."[2]

Few of the commentators considered the implications of their attacks. Taken at face value, they were suggesting that if I was asked who most influenced my thinking I should lie rather than run the risk of offending an agnostic, atheist, or someone of another faith by answering, "Christ."

More importantly, this elite opinion ignores a basic truth that I saw every day of the fourteen months I spent crisscrossing our country. The truth is simply this: Virtually every major problem that bedevils our country is, at its core, essentially a moral issue. For example, though we have passed hundreds of laws against racial discrimination, racial reconciliation still eludes us, and hate still resides in too many hearts. The daily headlines tell the story. In Texas, thugs dragged a black man behind their pickup truck until his body literally fell apart. The trial proved they were motivated by the color of their victim's skin. In northern Virginia, just a few miles from where I live, an African-American man stabbed an eight-year-old boy to death while shouting racist statements, according to eyewitnesses.

> **This elite opinion ignores a basic truth that I saw every day of the twelve months I spent crisscrossing our country: . . . Virtually every major problem that bedevils our country is, at its core, essentially a moral issue.**

We have produced more wealth for more people than any civilization in the history of the world, yet many of our children feel a spiritual emptiness that they try to fill with drugs, violence, or sex. Our medical technology has produced breakthroughs that enable us to operate on preborn children still in their mother's womb to correct heart defects and treat other conditions. But in the same hospital, the abortionist's tools are used on another floor to take the life of an unborn child.

Most Americans, regardless of their faith, know that these problems are overwhelmingly moral in nature. In fact, during the campaign, polling showed that two-thirds of the country thought the biggest problem facing America was not an economic crisis but a crisis of our heart and soul. Yet the elites in media, government, industry, and academia express foreboding when a political figure talks openly about faith or even discusses the issues facing the country in moral terms.

That's why I strongly felt that I had an obligation to make it clear that my faith would impact how I governed. As a conservative, I believe we should get rid of failed welfare programs; but as a Christian, I am obligated to find effective ways to help those who are in need. As a conservative, I disagree with racial quotas; but as a Christian, I am committed to work for racial reconciliation. My faith leads me to defend innocent human life, whether it is an unborn child, the disabled, or the sick.

RELIGIOUS DISCRIMINATION

I believe there is something else going on in this hostile reaction to the mention of faith, and it is simply this: bigotry. There are public attacks on evangelicals and Catholics that simply would not be tolerated against any other religious, ethnic, or political group. Governor Jesse "The Mind" (formerly "The Body") Ventura of Minnesota felt no hesitancy in telling *Playboy* magazine that organized Christianity "is a sham and a crutch for weak-minded people." Tell that to the missionaries, pastors, priests, and rank-and-file believers who rot in prisons and suffer torture and degradation at the hands of tyrants all over the world. These men and women aren't in show business or the mock exhibitions of the wrestling ring. What would the governor make of Dietrich Bonhoeffer and Martin Niemöller? Bonhoeffer was executed for his resistance to Nazi tyranny, and Niemöller, a decorated U-boat captain in World War I, survived imprisonment in a Nazi concentration camp. Both men's lives revolved around an abiding faith that required them to stand up against evil. I was so angered by Ventura's characterization of men and women of faith that I decided to go into his backyard to answer him. I promptly flew to Minnesota and held a press conference to suggest that a more accurate name for the Governor should be Jesse "The Bigot" Ventura. That same day the Minnesota Republican Convention held a presidential straw poll, which I won, narrowly defeating Bush.

But the hostility toward people of faith goes way beyond a loudmouthed governor. Art exhibits mock and desecrate the most sacred symbols worshiped by millions of Americans. The Brooklyn Museum of

Art displayed and defended an exhibit that featured the Virgin Mary surrounded by female genitalia and decorated with excrement. The exhibit is doubly offensive because the museum is funded by taxpayer money. Thus, Catholics are taxed in order to subsidize the mockery of their most cherished religious beliefs.

> According to the liberal elite, the Constitution does not permit a nativity scene to be displayed in the town square, but it does allow the desecration of religious symbols on public property paid for, in part, with taxpayer money.

So, according to the liberal elite, the Constitution does not permit a nativity scene to be displayed in the town square, but it does allow the desecration of religious symbols on public property paid for, in part, with taxpayer money. Apparently, if those impermissible nativity scenes were decorated with dung, they would be constitutional!

Unfortunately, the Brooklyn Museum exhibition wasn't an exception. At the University of North Carolina, the Ackland Art Museum featured a series of photographs entitled "Christ in New York." One showed a bearded man standing over the bloodied, partially naked body of a woman. The photo was titled "Christ Sees a Woman Who Has Died during an Illegal Abortion." This supposedly was a meditation on the political and social oppression of women fostered by the Catholic Church.

In Manchester, New Hampshire, in the respected Currier Gallery, a work was featured that caricatured and mocked the Eucharist. Called "Floor Show at the Last Supper," the painting featured frogs in bathing suits cavorting before the Lord's Table. By the way, the gallery is right across the street from the Chancery of the Diocese of Manchester.

The list goes on and on, from the play *Corpus Christi*, which depicted Christ as a homosexual having sex with his apostles, to a painting displayed at Penn State University showing a Nazi soldier and a Catholic priest standing side by side on top of a Jewish victim of the Holocaust.

And what is the reaction of the chattering class to all this—the people who make a living telling us what we are supposed to believe and think? They cite the Constitution and argue that the spirit of that document is violated when an avant-garde artist, poet, or playwright is criticized for mocking faith. Either way, believers get the short end of the stick.

I was so concerned about this bigotry that in the middle of the campaign I traveled to Saint Anselm College in Manchester, New Hampshire, to deliver a speech about it. Students and professors crowded into the student center to hear me speak on a cold New Hampshire evening. I told the crowd that the antireligious bigotry that is tolerated in our society is part of a larger hostility arising from radical secularists toward those institutions that stand in defense of Judeo-Christian moral values. The Catholic Church and evangelical Protestantism are the chief defenders of such values and ideals. These Christian institutions stand for the great moral traditions of Western civilization—marriage, the sacredness of sex within the institution of marriage, the sanctity of life in all its stages, and immutable standards of right and wrong.

The secularists know that the church and people of faith stand as the last obstacle to the final victory of radical, atheistic, and amoral secularism. This accounts for the rising hostility among American elites toward public expressions of traditional religion. The Left knows it must drive the church and Judeo-Christian values underground if radical secularism is to replace four thousand years of Western moral teaching.

And it is important to note that it is Catholics and evangelical Christians who are the targets of the secularists' attacks. Under the pretense of protecting the separation of church and state, many hysterically condemn the mixing of religion and politics. But this applies only if the religion is conservative Judeo-Christian. The cultural elite loses little sleep over the political activism of liberal churches and liberal clergymen. Only those who stand in defense of traditional moral values are singled out for bigoted attacks.

THE ABUSE OF THE FIRST AMENDMENT

This hostility toward religion—something that would have astounded and perplexed our Founding Fathers—accounts for the grotesquely distorted view of the First Amendment espoused by many on the extreme Left and the libertarian Right and unfortunately parroted by too many of our courts. The First Amendment's prohibition of the establishment of religion was intended to preserve and protect the free exercise of religion from the encroachments of government. Today, the establishment clause has been turned on its head and has become the enemy of Americans' right to freely exercise their faith.

In Pompano Beach, Florida, for example, the American Civil Liberties Union sued to stop a church from ringing its bells. It charged that exempting the church from the city's antinoise ordinance violated the separation of church and state. That was on Sunday mornings. On Saturday afternoons, the NCAA tried to stop college football players from praying, kneeling, or crossing themselves in

> The First Amendment's prohibition of the establishment of religion was intended to preserve and protect the free exercise of religion from the encroachments of government. Today, the establishment clause has been turned on its head and has become the enemy of Americans' right to freely exercise their faith.

the end zone after scoring a touchdown. Threatened with a lawsuit, the NCAA backed down.

Bigotry must be afforded no refuge in America. Anti-Catholicism has no place in our country or in the hearts of any people who call themselves Christian. Today Catholics and evangelicals must stand shoulder to shoulder in steadfast defense of those moral values that are under attack from the Left.

The growing acceptance of anti-Christian bigotry is a test for America. Silently accepting such bigotry and allowing people of faith to be driven from the public square would amount to a repudiation of our founding principle that God, not man, is the author of our rights.

> **Liberty untempered by virtue cannot survive, and a people who are not virtuous will not long remain free.**

We must ensure that Americans of all faiths will be able to acknowledge their Creator in public as the Founding Fathers did in our founding documents and public institutions. We must work for a country where reliable and traditional standards of right and wrong matter once again, where character and morality still count, where virtue is seen as something to treasure, indispensable to the preservation of liberty. Liberty untempered by virtue cannot survive, and a people who are not virtuous will not long remain free.

I will continue to protect religious expression and work to restore the freedom of the states to allow acknowledgment of God in public places. I will defend the rights of parents to guide their children's education and will work to ensure that every family has a choice of schools. And as I have done for the past twenty-five years, I will fight to make certain that every one of our children is welcomed into the world and protected by the law.

RELIGION AND PARTY POLITICS

Having said that, let me offer a caution about partisanship. Men and women of faith involved in government and politics do have a particular burden and a higher standard that must be followed. We must be careful not to shrink God to a mere "precinct worker" for either party. I am a Republican, but like all human institutions, the Republican Party is flawed. Neither party has a monopoly on virtue or vice. No American has to agree with each provision in the GOP platform in order to be a Christian. Some conservative Christians are Republicans because they see the party as being pro-life or in favor of traditional marriage. On the other hand, these same Christians look the other way when party officials don't make serious effort to do anything on those issues. Or they fail to speak up when the party puts trade in front of concern for the persecuted church. When Dick Cheney suggested in one of the debates that it would be OK if a state authorized same-sex marriage, I felt compelled to speak, and in fact, I wrote an editorial for the *New York Times* expressing my disappointment. How could I be silent when Cheney was taking the same position that I had frequently criticized when it was expressed by liberal Democrats? But I heard from many Christian Republicans who were angry that I had said anything, because they felt it helped the Democrats. One outraged woman asked me whether I understood that Cheney only gave that answer so he could be elected. Then she assured me he would do the right thing once elected. That would mean Cheney was being dishonest—hardly a tactic that Christians would want to embrace.

Many African-American Christians have decided their faith calls them to be Democrats because of that party's historical commitment to racial equality and its support of programs whose stated purpose is to help the poor. Yet they are silent when the national Democratic Party embraces the gay-rights agenda and blocks efforts to stop abortions even in the eighth or ninth month of pregnancy. And black church leaders were some of the most vocal defenders of Clinton's inexcusable behavior in the White House. Sure we are all sinners, but Clinton continued his behavior and deception for months. On the other hand, Christians in the GOP were tough on Clinton's conduct, but strangely silent when it came to disclosures about the personal behavior of some leading Republicans. Think how much better it would have been if Christian leaders, no matter what their party loyalty, had spoken with one voice on the fact that personal character had public consequences.

My point is simply this: Men and women of faith will accomplish nothing if we act like Republicans or Democrats first and believers second! Our priorities have to be the other way around if we want a more decent body politic. Otherwise, politics will transform us instead of us transforming politics. Secondly, politics is not a substitute for personal involvement in addressing the great problems of our country. Don't just vote pro-life—volunteer at a crisis pregnancy center, adopt a child, or become a foster parent. Don't just vote for welfare reform—make sure your church is involved in ministering to the poor, the homeless, and the aged. If people of faith in both parties do these things, we will, in fact, transform politics and the nation.

CHAPTER 8

CYNICISM

One of the most clever ads on television in 1999 was one by Monster.com, the on-line employment service. It featured children looking into the camera and saying things like, "When I grow up, I want to work long hours for low pay." The point, of course, is just the opposite — none of us wants to be taken advantage of in our jobs.

Green Party candidate Ralph Nader ran his own version of the ad during the final week of the 2000 campaign. It, too, showed children speaking directly into the camera, one at a time, with this message:

> When I grow up, I want the government to have the same problems
> it has today.
> I want to vote for the lesser of two evils.
> I want to be apathetic.
> I want tax breaks for the very rich.
> When I grow up, I want politicians to ignore me.

It was a funny, entertaining ad, but unfortunately it also reflects a basic truth.

American government and politics are desperately in need of reform. The widespread perception that the system is corrupt and that the special interests rule is feeding apathy, low voter turnout, and cynicism — all deadly characteristics in a democratic republic like the United States.

On the campaign trail, I ran into this pervasive cynicism all the time.

In Iowa, most of the farmers liked my message, but they had heard it all before. Politicians come into the state every four years before the caucuses, made big promises, and were never seen again. After a while, the people lose their faith that anyone in power will do anything to help them.

One farmer at an Iowa town meeting stood up with his seventeen-year-old son and told me the boy wanted to enlist in the army, "like I did when I was his age." But the father talked him out of it.

"I told him no one in Washington gives a damn about people like us. I don't want him fighting one of their wars," he said with a note of bitterness. A pretty extreme attitude, to be sure, but also a dire warning.

THE PROBLEM OF ABUNDANCE

The endless search for money to fund political campaigns adds to public cynicism, with each party pointing fingers at the other for scandals real and exaggerated. Many Republicans were amazed when there didn't seem to be much public reaction to Al Gore's campaign fundraiser at a Buddhist temple in California that violated several laws. But the main reason people yawned in reaction to the story is the widespread belief that everyone does it. Even news of money flowing indirectly from the Chinese government into Bill Clinton's 1996 reelection campaign caused barely a ripple with average voters.

Today's political parties will go anywhere to get the money they need to win, and both sides are afraid of any reform that may give one of them advantage over the other. No wonder the public becomes cynical when they see the leadership of the Democrat Party constantly rail against the tobacco industry, then discover that the Democrat Governors Association accepted sixty thousand dollars from that industry in the last three months before the 2000 election.

My party relies on millions of voters who want a return to traditional

> **Today's political parties will go anywhere to get the money they need to win, and both sides are afraid of any reform that may give one of them advantage over the other.**

values. Many of those voters are engaged in brutal battles to stop the expansion of casinos, lotteries, and video gambling in their states. They do so because they know the social costs of widespread and easily available gambling options — addiction, family breakup, bankruptcies, spousal abuse, and the undermining of values like thrift. But that didn't stop some Republican congressional leaders from holding fund-raisers in Las Vegas casinos. A National Gambling Commission was created by the Congress to satisfy social conservatives, but the commission was toothless and had no legal authority, largely because of pressure put on the Republican leadership by Frank Farenkopf, former chairman of the Republican National Committee, now the top lobbyist for the gaming industry in Washington.

Al Gore and Joe Lieberman denounced the negative impact of Hollywood on our children and told parents they would be on their side. Within days, they went to Hollywood, raised millions from the industry they had just criticized, privately reassured Hollywood that no serious regulation would result, then seemed surprised when millions of people concluded that no politician is going to bite the hand that feeds him.

This influence of big money is felt at the state level too. A few years ago, voters in California were given a chance to pass a referendum that required English to be emphasized in the schools' bilingual classes. The referendum passed and it is working well, with new research showing that language-minority children are learning faster and improving their test scores. The odd thing was that both major-party candidates for governor and lieutenant governor put together a joint ad — against the reform! Later it was discovered that all four campaigns had received large donations from the wealthy owner of a Spanish-speaking TV station, who had a vested interest in Hispanic kids not learning English quickly because it could threaten his business! Fortunately, this special interest was defeated by the voice of the people that time.

The impulse toward reform is powerful among average Americans, even if it grows dim in Washington. When my party took control of the Congress in 1994 for the first time in decades, our Contract with America included a commitment to term limits. Many of the candidates promised, if elected, to limit themselves by not standing for reelection after six years. After all, this followed the intent of the founders, who envisioned citizen legislators who would serve their country for a season but not become career politicians. However, once elected, their tune changed. Congress brought up several different term-limit measures, allowing everyone to vote for one version or another, but ensuring that none of them would receive sufficient votes to actually become law. By the 2000 election, a number of the "reformer" members of Congress had experienced a change of heart about voluntarily not running for reelection. They now had the power of incumbency on their side, and they weren't going to give it up. So much for the Contract with America.

There are exceptions, of course. My good friend Congressman Tom Coburn of Oklahoma said he would step down after three terms, and he did so in 2000. Tom believes that long years in office inevitably result in the best men and women becoming part of the problem rather than part of the solution. Ultimately they forget the values of the people who elected them. Even during his six years in Congress, Tom guarded against that risk by returning home every weekend to continue his medical practice and do what he loves most, deliver babies. I have no doubt that Tom would have been reelected from his conservative Oklahoma district in 2000, and probably for many years after. But he made a promise and he kept it.

It is also no coincidence that time after time, Congressman Coburn took to the floor of the house to fight against pork-barrel spending, the practice that wastes millions of tax dollars in each congressional district for dubious projects, at best. Many congressmen are elected on promises of controlling spend-

> **Time and again entrepreneurs and independent business owners told me they would be bankrupt or in jail if they ran their businesses or abused their customers the way Washington does.**

ing, but only a few remain committed to their promises when their own reelection is at stake.

Average Americans want good economic policies and fiscal discipline. Time and again entrepreneurs and independent business owners told me they would be bankrupt or in jail if they ran their businesses or abused their customers the way Washington does. That's why they vote for candidates who promise to control the growth of government and to stop bureaucratic fraud and abuse. That's why they want people in office who are committed to tax cuts and simplification of the tax code. They want political leadership that actually means it when it says, "Read my lips—no new taxes." And that's why the ranks of the cynical and the turned-off grow with each election.

LESS THAN MEETS THE EYE

I began this chapter by talking about a Nader ad that featured children. And it is our children and the growing cynicism among them that has me most concerned. At every school I visited during my campaign there were a few kids who cared passionately; some agreed with me and others were opposed. But friend or foe, I was inspired by their interest in their country and its future.

The overwhelming majority of kids, however, expressed the cynicism we normally associate with a life of disappointment, broken promises, and crushed dreams. I considered it a great victory when we could turn these kids on, and I did time and time again. I took them seriously. I didn't tell them what they wanted to hear, and I didn't try to act like I had all the answers. I spoke out against drug legalization in schools where many kids thought marijuana use should be penalty free. I told them they would be better off with student loans instead of grants, because you appreciate something more when you pay for it instead of having someone else foot the bill. I also appealed to their hearts and told them that they should devote part of their lives to something bigger than their own self-interest by helping the poor, feeding the hungry, tutoring a younger child, cleaning up their community, or serving their country in the military.

By the time I left a school, kids would be scrambling for bumper and lapel stickers. We won the first major straw vote of the 2000 presidential contest at the Conservative Political Action Committee convention in Washington, besting all the other big names, largely because hundreds of college kids drove for hours to vote for me.

> **Government will always be important. Today it just isn't as ennobling as it once was, because those who run for office are seldom willing or capable of inspiring us in an age of polls, consultants, and imagemakers.**

This is what the politics of my youth was like. In the 1960s and 1970s, kids and adults believed something big was at stake in whom we chose as leaders. Richard Nixon and John F. Kennedy drew mammoth crowds in major cities. The emotional reactions they received then are now reserved for rock stars and athletes. Some of my conservative friends think this is a good thing, that it is a sign that government is less and less

important in our lives. But government will always be important.
Today it just isn't as ennobling as it
once was, because those who run
for office are seldom willing or
capable of inspiring us in an age
of polls, consultants, and image-
makers.

> Ronald Reagan had a
> motto on his desk in the
> Oval Office that simply
> said, "There is no limit
> to what you can accom-
> plish if you don't mind
> who gets the credit."

I believe people are tired of the
values of Washington, D.C. In this
city everyone wants to take the credit when something goes well, but
every bad idea and every failed government program is an "orphan."
Ronald Reagan had a motto on his desk in the Oval Office that simply
said, "There is no limit to what you can accomplish if you don't mind
who gets the credit." He believed it and governed with that thought in
mind, but he was the exception. Here, there is a whole industry—public relations, image molders, consultants, press manipulators, and political handlers—that operates on the exact opposite philosophy, devoted
to making you appear bigger and more important than you really are.

For eight years we had an administration that perfected not taking
responsibility for its actions. Lies were defended with statements such
as, "It all depends what the meaning of 'is' is," or, "There is no controlling legal authority."

Ironically, those same politicians took responsibility for things they
had nothing to do with. Former President Clinton told the country time
and time again that he had "given" us the greatest economic expansion
since the end of World War II. I thought that expansion was the result
of the energy, intelligence, hard work, and risk taking of the workers,
investors, entrepreneurs, innovators, and families of America. What
hubris to think that a politician is more central to the growth of the
economy than the people who drive it every day with their brains and

the sweat of their brows. One thing is certain, though politicians will argue about who is responsible for our economic growth, they will not run to the microphone to take any responsibility the next time the economy turns down, as it inevitably will.

Voters are hungry for accountability. When Republicans took control of the Congress in 1994, I suggested a simple idea to Newt Gingrich, then Speaker of the House of Representatives. Instead of another pay raise for members of Congress, I suggested Newt call a press conference and say something like this: "We are going to cut Congressional salaries 10 percent. We are asking you to tighten your belt and we should be willing to do the same. We will put the money from the salary cut in escrow. Two years from now, look at what we have done. If we kept our promise to make fundamental reform and change the way business is done in Washington, you can renew our contract by reelecting a Republican Congress. Then and only then will we take a pay increase." Newt looked at me as if I had just landed from Mars, and the idea went nowhere.

In every election since then, the Republican majority in the House of Representatives has decreased. Attempts to get rid of government bureaucracy failed, and Gingrich eventually became a liability in the eyes of the general public.

Could it have been different? I think so. In the rest of America, employees are rewarded when they do a job well, and they are penalized when they fail to complete their assignments. Even a child understands that. When I brought up this pay-for-performance approach on the campaign trail, it always brought a roar of approval from the crowd.

C. William Pollard, chairman of the ServiceMaster Company, wrote a runaway bestseller, *The Soul of the Firm*, in which he outlines his philosophy of leadership that is built on his strong Christian faith. He writes, "Will the leader please stand up? Not the president, but the role model. Not the highest paid person in the firm, but the risk taker.

Not the person with the most perks, but the servant. Not the person who promotes himself, but the promoter of others. Not the administrator, but the initiator. Not the taker, but the giver. Not the talker, but the listener.

> **Without a greater ennobling purpose, this "shining city on a hill" will not inspire our children, nor will it be a force for good in the world.**

People working together to perform a common objective need and want effective leadership—leadership they can trust—leadership that will nurture the soul."[1] Well said!

Our souls are nurtured first and foremost in our families, our places of worship, and in relationships with friends and loved ones. Government cannot and should not be a substitute for these things. But our political leadership and politics can nurture our souls too, by calling us to great national endeavors that are bigger than our individual self-interests. And if America is going to be something more than mere accumulations of wealth, we'd better get such leadership soon. Without a greater ennobling purpose, this "shining city on a hill" will not inspire our children, nor will it be a force for good in the world.

The legal wrangling and lawsuits that erupted between the two presidential candidates after election night 2000 was the last thing the country needed. Serious doubts about the fairness and accuracy of our elections have now been placed in the minds of millions of citizens. Stories of homeless people being recruited in Wisconsin and voting in exchange for cigarettes, polling places in Missouri being kept open extra hours in areas that favored one party, and in Florida, vote counting . . . and recounting . . . and recounting in an effort to produce the result each side wanted—all these served to undermine confidence in our political process. If in the future election night becomes the starting point for legal maneuvering to win in the courts what has not been won at the ballot box, our country will be the worse for it.

I hope and pray that our new president will find a way to call our youth to a higher standard again. There are great causes and great needs to be met on issues ranging from racial reconciliation to how we can empower average Americans to take responsibility for their communities and neighborhoods. There is a desperate need for reform of our schools, our tax systems, and our healthcare system. There are injustices to address, liberty to defend, and discoveries to be made. Government, properly utilized, can be a force for reform, and I am committed to making sure it is just that. But while we are trying to get government on the right page, many Americans are going forward on their own to deal with the problems facing our country. I saw the results of their efforts in every community I visited. I want to tell you about some of these people and what they are doing for our country.

CHAPTER 9

THE VOLUNTEER
SPIRIT

To listen to the debate in Washington, you would think that without government programs and bureaucracy no hungry person would be fed, no homeless person would sleep under a roof, and no addict would be cured in America. The reality is that many of the most important things that happen in our country each day are done by volunteers and private organizations. Drive-by shootings, dishonest politicians, ripoff artists, and the me-first folks among us dominate the nightly news, but the countless acts of just plain folks done out of love, compassion, and a call to service are all too often relegated to the back pages of our papers, if they make it in at all.

As I traveled the country, I met scores of individuals who follow the advice of a popular bumper sticker that says, "Practice countless acts of random kindness." Americans are actively mentoring young Americans: providing a child with someone to help with homework, cheer on the sidelines, and make the rugged and increasingly treacherous journey of growing up a bit easier. It has been said that every child needs someone who is crazy about them, who puts them first before anything else. These mentors, from Midwest truckdrivers to Wall Street lawyers, are doing just that for kids who might otherwise slip through the cracks.

Other Americans have stepped up to help the poor and the homeless, as the federal government has ended programs that appeared to be hurting the poor more than helping them. Millions of Americans are proving that person-to-person ministry to the poor is more effective than

Washington programs, with a surplus of paid bureaucrats and a shortage of real compassion.

> **All of us at the end of the day want the same things: a chance for a decent life, a roof over our heads, a loving family, and a better life for our children than we had.**

The Bauer family spent Thanksgiving Day in 1999 off the campaign trail at the Central Union Mission in the inner city of Washington, D.C. We spent hours talking with the homeless and finding out what had happened in their lives to bring them to the difficult times they were experiencing. Many of the men were wrestling with drug and alcohol problems. Some had merely fallen on hard times, and some had been raised in dysfunctional and abusive families. Many were abandoned by their fathers and raised by single mothers, who were on crack or were prostitutes themselves. As we sat and talked with them, I was reminded again that all of us at the end of the day want the same things: a chance for a decent life, a roof over our heads, a loving family, and a better life for our children than we had. Later that evening, as our family gathered for our own Thanksgiving meal, we were more acutely aware of our blessings than perhaps ever before.

CARE FOR CRISIS PREGNANCIES

Everyone knows we should help the homeless, but there is no such consensus on abortion. The abortion debate is probably the most contentious and divisive issue in American public life. I am unambiguous in my deeply held belief that America will never be what our founders hoped unless all of our children are welcomed into the world and protected by the law. This debate will continue to rage, but while it does, hundreds of thousands of Americans put their time and resources where their mouths are, by supporting and volunteering at crisis pregnancy centers (CPCs) around the country.

> **I am unambiguous in my deeply held belief that America will never be what our founders hoped unless all of our children are welcomed into the world and protected by the law.**

If you want to know who the most forgotten volunteers are, you don't have to look any further than these CPCs. Day after day they make themselves available to girls and women from twelve to fifty who are pregnant, abandoned, afraid, and in many cases, without hope. They minister to them, love them unconditionally, pray with them, cry with them, and most importantly, show them that there are better solutions than taking the life of the innocent child inside of them. Many of the counselors and volunteers I met around the country have experienced abortion themselves, and they are now committed to helping other women avoid the experience that takes the life of one human being, the unborn child, and wounds another human being, the mother.

There are thousands of CPCs, from one end of the country to the other. They operate on shoestring budgets. The government indirectly subsidizes abortion clinics all over the country, but CPCs and the big-hearted people who work in them are usually on their own. For years I have tried to do my part to help them by speaking at fund-raising dinners all across the country. I never cease to be amazed at the dedication and selflessness of the people I meet at these events. The battles in Washington make the headlines, but CPC volunteers can look at a one-year-old child and know that without their dedication and open hearts, that baby would not have lived.

The dedicated staffs at CPCs give lie to the charge that pro-life advocates only care about children before they are born, not afterward. They provide clothing, job opportunities, diapers, baby food, and day-to-day resources for the women who make the courageous choice of life for their babies.

The late John Cardinal O'Connor of New York repeatedly offered in public that the Catholic Church would take care of any woman who chose life for her child. The offer was real, but it didn't stop the *New York Times* from promoting the myth of uncaring pro-lifers.

By the way, the work of CPCs in helping women choose life has become much more effective since the widespread availability of sonogram machines. Once expectant mothers are able to actually see the life inside of them, they seldom choose to end it. Seeing your baby's heartbeat or a small thumb being sucked by an unborn child blows away the idea it is merely a blob of tissue. But ultrasound machines cost money, many thousands of dollars per machine. They are well beyond the reach of the budgets of most crisis pregnancy centers. During my campaign, I repeatedly promised to start a federal program to provide sonogram machines for every CPC in the country. That simple step would do more to save real children than most of the multibillion-dollar boondoggles that Washington has established in the last thirty years.

HEALING SEGREGATION

For decades now, from the civil rights movement led by Martin Luther King Jr. right up to the present day, America has tried by law to stop racial discrimination and reach our shared dream of racial reconciliation. Yet with all our work, the divisions between us remain large and unbridged. Many of the laws passed have been essential to a fair and decent society, but others have perversely increased racial bigotry. Here, too, the best work being done in the country isn't being done by senators, congressmen, or presidents. Instead, volunteers working in churches and community organizations are bringing people together and breaking through racial stereotypes.

Unfortunately, one of the most segregated days in America has been Sunday. But from one end of the country to the other, suburban white churches and urban black churches are breaking down the barriers, joining

> **America has tried by law to stop racial discrimination and reach our shared dream of racial reconciliation. Yet with all our work, the divisions between us remain large and unbridged.**

together for worship services and to talk through some of the problems that keep us apart. Groups like Promise Keepers bring together men of all races and unite them by reminding them they are brothers, because they are all God's children. My son, Zachary, and I attended the incredible Standing in the Gap March in Washington on October 4, 1997. We watched men of every race and ethnicity pray fervently for America's future and ask forgiveness for the sin of racial hatred and bigotry. The healing done on the Washington Mall that day, largely ignored by the city's political establishment, dwarfs the pages of legislation and regulation that have been passed in an effort to end our racial divide.

HOPE FOR ADDICTION

In 1969, an incredible movie was released entitled *The Cross and the Switchblade*. Starring Pat Boone and Erik Estrada, the movie told the real-life story of pastor David Wilkerson and his ministry to lost teenagers. Today Wilkerson's ministry, an international drug-rehabilitation program called Teen Challenge, has one of the highest success rates anywhere in the world. I'm convinced it works because it does what government can't or won't—it ministers to people's souls, not just their drug- and alcohol-addicted bodies.

> [Teen Challenge] works because it does what government can't or won't—it ministers to people's souls, not just their drug- and alcohol-addicted bodies.

A few days before the Iowa caucuses, I found time to visit the Teen Challenge in Colfax, Iowa. It was a visit I'll never forget. Surrounded by a dozen reporters and cameras, I met Rev. Warren Hunsberger, the executive director of the facility and a man who has devoted his life to serving others. Warren and his wife, Gay, have seven children, and the whole family lives at the center, ministering to men recovering from addictions.

In my years in and out of government, I have toured thousands of schools, clinics, drug centers, hospitals, retirement homes, factories, and homes. After a while, I found that I could tell if a place was working just by walking in the front door and looking around. There is a feel about success and seriousness of purpose that permeates the atmosphere. I have seen and felt it in inner-city schools and suburban health clinics, and I could see and feel it in the first few minutes in this Teen Challenge facility. Everything I saw and heard in the next hour confirmed that first impression.

Hunsberger showed me around the campus, then he got the men together in the chapel to meet with me. Most of the men probably didn't know me, and I doubt that politics was a high priority for them. I'm sure they assumed that it would be hard for some guy from Washington to have any idea what they were dealing with in their lives. And since I was a Republican candidate, wearing a suit and surrounded by attentive aides and cameras, most of them probably thought I was born with a silver spoon in my mouth. I knew if I was going to have a chance to know their hearts, they first had to know mine.

I talked with them about the mean streets where I grew up, about the rampant alcoholism, family breakdown, crime, and corruption that prevailed in my hometown. I told them about the open prostitution and strip joints and the bars on every corner that enticed the men on Friday nights, and how many of those men lost their paychecks for the week before they ever got home. I told them I could have been drawn into the same things if Christ hadn't come into my life.

I could see the barriers dropping as I talked. Suddenly, I wasn't just a politician from Washington. I was a real person who had experienced firsthand the same problems they wrestled with. The men began to tell me their stories, and I was reminded once again that governing means nothing if it isn't about real flesh and blood.

Lloyd Johnston was one of the young men who gave his testimony. Lloyd never met his biological father; he was in prison when Lloyd was born. His stepfather was initially an avowed atheist, but later became a Christian and eventually a pastor. Nonetheless, Lloyd struggled with demons in his own life. He told me he had spent twenty-two years "in bondage to alcoholism, drugs, and pornography."

"Mr. Bauer, during those years I lost a lot of things: cars, motor-cycles, a house, friends, relationships, a successful delivery business, and worst of all, I was lost. My bondage has taken me many places, including jail, five rehabilitation centers, and even a psychiatric ward."

Finally, Lloyd said that he repented, accepted Christ, and turned his life around, and that "instantly" he was free "of the compulsions that have plagued me for the past twenty-two years."

There weren't many dry eyes in the room while Lloyd spoke. Nearly every man there that morning had incredible stories of drug addiction, child abuse, alcoholism, pornography, sexual addictions, and rejection. And every one had a story that made it clear they were able to heal their bodies only after their hearts and souls had been healed.

As I met these men, I wondered how many times it was assumed they were lost causes. By conventional measure, a lot of the men that day should have been written off as hopeless years ago. Some had criminal records or had been severe discipline problems in school. They were antisocial, and some were violent. But America can't afford to leave any more people behind.

> **As I met these men, I wondered how many times it was assumed they were lost causes.**

The experience of those men in Teen Challenge is not unusual. Research is now overwhelming that faith-based programs work best in dealing with lost people. Whether it is the success of Chuck Colson's Prison Fellowship or success in getting and keeping people off welfare, these programs do what government cannot.

A consensus is building in favor of faith-based approaches, but there is a need for caution. Courts continue to be hostile to any tax money flowing to faith-based programs. Even worse, if government did subsidize these programs, it could be at the cost of the religious core that is essential to their approach and the secret of their success in the first place!

President Bush deserves credit for his faith-based initiative. I believe that with appropriate safeguards written into the law we can help these most effective groups while protecting them from government interference.

These are serious considerations, but one thing is clear: We won't be able to help our hurting neighbors if they don't understand that God loves them and that they are His unique creation.

CHAPTER 10

---✸✸✸---

THE ELDERLY

The two of them were quietly eating lunch in a more private corner of the restaurant on one of New Hampshire's picturesque main streets. The noonhour rush was over, and they seemed to be enjoying the relative quiet that had descended on the dining room. I'm sure they didn't want to be noticed, but they couldn't help but notice me as Carol and I came in the front door followed by our kids, campaign aides, a TV crew, several local newspaper reporters, and an Associated Press photographer who shot pictures everywhere we went. I was in the middle of another day campaigning in the state's picture-postcard towns, introducing myself to strangers, asking voters what issues concerned them, shaking hands, moving on to the next table, the next store, the next town. Normally I tried to avoid people who through their body language let me know they clearly didn't want to be bothered, but on this particular day, as I went to meet the other diners, my glance kept going back to those two quietly eating their lunch.

They were "seasoned" Americans, probably in their early seventies. He was seated in a chair, and she sat across from him at the table in a wheelchair. Several napkins had been tucked into her blouse to catch the food that dropped from her shaking hand. Her lips drooped slightly on one side, the evidence of a recent stroke.

When my family and I neared their table, the gentleman quickly stood up and offered his hand. I introduced my family to them, and soon we were talking about the challenges they faced because of declin-

> "We worked hard all our lives, we paid our taxes, but now when we are in trouble, we feel forgotten and ignored. All the politicians do is yell at each other. We can't even figure out who is on our side."

ing health. They had been healthy all their working lives and had retired to enjoy each other in their twilight years. On vacation in Florida one Saturday morning he awoke, startled by something. He discovered that his wife had suffered a stroke in her sleep. Now the love of his life could not dress herself or bathe or get around on her own. He was doing the best he could to care for her, but it was becoming more difficult with each passing day. For a time they had been able to get home healthcare. A visiting nurse came in the mornings to help him get his wife up and about, but with recent budget cuts, Medicare no longer covered this service. His own failing health, including arthritis and back problems, made it virtually impossible for him to do the job alone, and they had no relatives nearby.

But with all of this, they did not complain. In fact, when we first began our conversation, his dear wife apologized to Carol and me because of how she looked.

"I'm a mess," she said. "I'm sorry there is food all over my napkin. I'm embarrassed by how I look. I'm trying the best I can."

"You're sorry? Ma'am, you have nothing to apologize for. All I see is an incredibly courageous woman out with her husband having lunch. You are doing great. I can tell you are a fighter. I am amazed you are eating this well and talking so well after your stroke. We should apologize to you for interrupting your time together. The last thing you probably wanted today was to spend time with a political candidate," I responded.

"Is there anything you could do to help people like us," she asked, "if you were elected president? We worked hard all our lives, we paid our taxes, but now when we are in trouble, we feel forgotten and ignored. All the politicians do is yell at each other. We can't even figure out who is on our side." *Is this how those in public life appear to the average senior voter?* I couldn't help but wonder.

Her husband shook his head. "I just don't know how much longer I can handle her without help," he said. His face showed the strain of what they had been through.

And what about the answer to her question? Was there something I could do to help them if I was the president? Or did the last thirty years teach us that government inevitably makes things worse. It tries to help the poor and ends up trapping them in poverty. It promises healthcare reform, but so distorts the marketplace that prices are higher than before.

All over the country I met people worried about and struggling with the high costs of prescription drugs. I talked to Americans who actually had to choose each month between getting the medicines they needed and buying enough food. Others were watching as a lifetime of savings slowly evaporated before their eyes. Too often, the members of our greatest generation, who won wars and came back from financial ruin, were having to swallow their pride and turn to family for help or keep their pride intact and forgo medications.

No wonder there is a political payoff for liberal politicians who rail against the drug companies. They are hitting a nerve for millions of Americans. My Republican Party received millions of dollars in campaign donations from the big drug companies because our conservative candidates defended them. They argued that the marketplace sets the price of drugs and that taxpayers shouldn't have to subsidize someone else's medical bills. I have friends and neighbors who have been on both sides of this debate, depending on where they were in life at the time.

THE BIG BUSINESS OF HEALTHCARE

I refuse to believe that these two choices—government-run prescription drug programs or an unfettered marketplace—are the only two choices we have. Instead, real reform of our system can help us reach a goal that would please the overwhelming majority of us.

First, let's stop demonizing the drug companies. The fact is that these American companies are producing more wonder drugs to treat everything from high cholesterol to cancer than any other companies or governments in the world. Deadly diseases have been tamed, years have been added to life expectancy, and suffering has been lessened.

> **It has been estimated that for every five thousand potential new medications that are tested in labs, on average, three will get as far as actual clinical trials to prove their worth. And of those three, one will be approved by government regulators for human use.**

Are the drugs expensive? Yes, in some cases obscenely so. For the uninsured, the drugs are a mocking possibility, tantalizing but out of reach. Drug company profitability is higher than the average U.S. industry, and stockholders in U.S. drug companies have done well as a result. But don't forget this is a risk-based industry. It has been estimated that for every five thousand potential new medications that are tested in labs, on average, three will get as far as actual clinical trials to prove their worth. And of those three, one will be approved by government regulators for human use, a process that can take an average of fifteen years to complete. The profits on that one approved drug have to recoup all the lost investment for the medications that were researched but never made it to the finish line, and produce enough profits to keep shareholders happy and provide for new research. It's a tall order.

So, when a big government politician begins to talk about regulating prices for the drugs—direct or indirect price controls—you should get nervous. Translation: Price controls mean less research, and less research means fewer breakthroughs on drugs that you or I or someone we love may need, if not today then tomorrow. Act recklessly in Washington, and we could destroy an industry that is making incredible medical breakthroughs.

Most of the people I met on the campaign trail understood that. Some were unhappy and frustrated with cost issues. But they were hesitant, fearing that Washington would make problems worse.

Does that mean there is nothing that can and should be done? Absolutely not. The fact is that those great drug companies I just defended will in fact make very penny they can and charge as much as they can because the goal of a corporation is profit. A free society will allow free enterprise to flourish. But a decent society, which we are, will look for ways to level the playing field so that exploitation is restrained and all its people have the best chance possible to get good healthcare.

Generic drugs have been a godsend. For years, consumers' only choices were brand-name medications developed by big drug companies. But in 1984, when I worked in the White House Office of Policy Development, a law was passed and signed by President Ronald Reagan that guaranteed cheaper, generic versions of medications could be quickly brought to the marketplace. The law allows the brand-name drug to be sold exclusively for a reasonable length of time so that a profit can be made. Then generic companies are permitted to sell their version of the medication when the original patent expires. The result is a drastic decline in prices for the patient.

Great idea, but it is an idea being undermined by greed. Large pharmaceutical companies have perfected a hundred different legal maneuvers to delay the competition for their brand-name drugs.

Courtroom legal maneuvers are becoming more important than medical research in developing new drugs. It happened in the middle of the presidential campaign when Bristol-Myers Squibb blocked a little generic company, IVAX Corporation, from bringing out a cheaper version of Taxol, an anticancer drug. Bristol-Myers Squibb sells $3 million of Taxol a day, and profit margins are estimated at 90 percent. They tried every legal maneuver possible to delay IVAX's drug from reaching the market, preventing cancer patients from getting the drug for a third less. An analyst for a Wall Street firm summed up the feelings of a lot of fair-minded people when he said of the Bristol-Myers Squibb maneuverings, "These are people with second, third, and fourth mortgages on their houses to pay for this. This isn't a cough medicine. These people are dying." I strongly support legislation pending in Congress that will stop the makers of brand-name drugs from filing frivolous patents on nonessential items such as tablet size—a tactic that is being used to delay the approval of such drugs and, thus, inhibit competition. Drug companies deserve time to make a reasonable profit, but generic companies must be encouraged and protected as they bring those drugs to the general public at more reasonable costs. Republicans and Democrats should be able to agree on this simple reform. But like all reform in Washington, it will be a brutal battle, and massive soft-money donations by the big drug companies to both parties will make it harder than it should be to accomplish.

What about HMOs? Republicans tend to be pro-HMO and Democrats demonize them. I often heard horror stories on the campaign trail of care denied or diagnostic tests postponed or disallowed in the desire to control costs. That's reasonable, unless it is your cancer that wasn't diagnosed in time or your heart attack that wasn't prevented.

In the old system, all of the inducements were to order tests and treatments as long as insurance covered them. That wasn't working and it drove up healthcare costs for everyone. But now the pendulum has swung in the opposite direction. Accountants are making decisions that only doctors should make. To the HMO, the patient with chronic illness is all too often seen only as a bottom-line liability.

> **Accountants are making decisions that only doctors should make. To the HMO, the patient with chronic illness is all too often seen only as a bottom-line liability.**

I support a reasonable patient's bill of rights. Lawyers seldom make things better, but an HMO bureaucrat needs to know that cost-driven treatment decisions that are inappropriate medically are unacceptable. I don't like bureaucracy, period. I don't like government bureaucrats who can't think outside the box. And I don't like HMO bureaucrats looking over doctors' shoulders. And I don't see why one set of bureaucrats is preferable to another.

My mother may be a lot like yours. She often doesn't understand the medical jargon and the treatment appropriate for her. It is too easy for an HMO to cut corners and protect profits at her expense. If their discretion or misconduct results in harm to her, on what principle of justice or decency would some argue that she should have no redress in court? I don't want trial lawyers descending like vultures on HMOs. But a reasonable right to sue makes sense, with ceilings on awards and appropriate just remedies, and it would empower her as health issues grow in importance in her life.

THE TRUTH ABOUT SOCIAL SECURITY

Social Security is another issue that generates a lot of heat and very little light. Liberals present themselves as the protectors of the program and say conservatives will threaten it. But both sides know the demographic facts of life. When my parents first married and Dad was working sixty-hour weeks, there were ten workers for every one recipient. But as the baby boomers age, the ratio is approaching two-to-one. Either the program must be reformed or the tax burden will break the backs of younger workers.

I ran television ads in Iowa that featured the most important older American in my life, my own mom. We filmed it back in Newport, Kentucky, in the living room of the home I lived in from the second grade until I left to go to college. You can imagine how nervous she was. I do television all the time, but for my mother this was a first. Mom is a meticulous housekeeper and likes everything in its place, but the film crew turned our living room into a shambles with cameras, lights, screens, and monitors. Plus, poor Mom had no idea that you can't get away with saying your lines one time. We probably filmed that ad thirty-five times before she finally announced that she had had enough—the filming was over!

The commercial featured the two of us talking about Social Security. At the end, I promised to protect it and Mom chimed in with, "You better too!" The "threat" was clear: If I didn't, I would hear from my mother! The ad caused a lot of talk in Iowa, and it came up in every nursing home and retirement village I visited.

Few issues better illustrate the problem in Washington than does Social Security. My dad worked for forty-five years, and every week payroll taxes were taken out of his check and paid into the Social Security system. Dad believed that those taxes were going into an account with his name on it and that Washington was faithfully investing his money. He has since passed away, and my mother continues to receive the monthly check that Dad wanted her to have.

But my father would be shocked, and so would millions of other Americans today, if he knew what has really been happening to Social Security money. In 1983, Social Security taxes were raised by 25 percent, and they have continued to go up—a tremendous burden on today's workers. Those tax increases have created an exploding surplus in Social Security. For this year, it is estimated at $156 billion. But that money wasn't invested. Instead, politicians from both parties have been spending it for years on dozens of programs that have nothing to do with the eld-

> My father would be shocked, and so would millions of other Americans today, if he knew what has really been happening to Social Security money. . . . Politicians from both parties have been spending it for years on dozens of programs that have nothing to do with the elderly or the disabled.

erly or the disabled. In place of the $156 billion, there are bonds or IOUs, and no one has any idea how those obligations are going to be met.

Are you sitting down? Since 1983, $105 trillion has been taken from Social Security and spent by the politicians for their favorite programs. Fifteen years from now, less money will be coming into Social Security than is being paid out, and there will be a day of reckoning.[1]

But it gets worse. The debt that is in the Social Security fund in the form of IOUs is being counted by Washington as if it were cash, and it is the major portion of the so-called surplus that both parties took credit for in last year's election campaign. Some courageous politicians have spoken up, but they are drowned out by the rest of their party's elected officials. Senator Ernest Hollings (D-SC) said the Social Security money has been looted. Senator Daniel Patrick Moynihan (D-NY) and Senator Robert Kerry (D-MA) introduced a bill that would separate Social Security from the rest of the budget, so that spend-happy politicians couldn't get their sweaty hands on it. But of course, it will never get out of committee on Capitol Hill. If it did, 80 percent of our current budget surplus would disappear and neither Bush nor Gore would

> **The debt that is in the Social Security fund in the form of IOUs is being counted by Washington as if it were cash, and it is the major portion of the so-called surplus that both parties took credit for in last year's election campaign.**

have been able to propose all their great ideas of how to spend it—for you, of course!

The big theme in Republican circles right now to deal with these issues is privatization of Social Security. The idea is that workers will be allowed to put a percentage of their payroll taxes into certain authorized stocks and bonds and, according to the advocates, get a better return for their retirement.

What's not clear is how this change would be paid for. Seniors like my mother get a monthly benefit that comes from the taxes paid by current workers. If we are going to keep our promises to current retirees and those about to retire, as we surely will, we will have to dip into general revenues to make up for the money invested in the stock market!

I don't like government picking the stocks we can invest in. And I don't like being required to put the money in stocks alone. What about taking a portion of Social Security taxes and investing it in our children or family now by investing in human capital? Privatization raises a lot of questions that I believe argue for caution.

I am an unapologetic conservative, but I think programs like Social Security have been good. For my mother's generation, trying to recover from the Great Depression, Social Security was a godsend, and in neighborhoods like the one I grew up in, many of the elderly would be living in poverty if it weren't for Social Security. Most people don't know it, but Social Security is one of the last federal programs that is actually biased toward the traditional family. Elderly women, like my mother, who were full-time homemakers and did not work in a paid job outside the home, actually receive a higher survivor's benefit than they would have otherwise.

We can reform Social Security and develop a more equitable health-care system. There are solutions that avoid massive increases in the size of government and the number of bureaucrats. There are approaches that will keep the promises that have been made between the generations. But if we are going to find those solutions, we first have to insist that the politicians stop using half-truths and frightening the elderly. And we must remember that in a decent society, as rich as ours, there is no reason to leave anyone behind.

Chapter 11

THE PLIGHT OF THE FAMILY FARMER

I went all over Iowa to introduce myself to the voters—to coffee shops and city parks, local schools and church socials. The audiences were often filled with hardworking farm families on the edge of bankruptcy. These good folks were walking a tightrope over an abyss of falling farm prices, broken promises from the politicians in Washington, rising interest rates, and increasingly unfair competition from large corporate farms.

I remember one particular morning, we were in a small main-street coffee shop packed with people: moms with their kids, a local schoolteacher, quite a few retired folks, local party volunteers, and businessmen and women. Politics in Iowa, like New Hampshire, is all "retail": People want to look you in the eye and take the measure of you.

On this morning, as on most mornings, there were a number of farm families present. I made a few remarks and opened up the event to questions. A farmer in the front raised his hand right away.

I don't remember his name now, but I saw and talked to him and his "brothers" all over the state. He was a big man, with the weathered skin of someone who works outside for a living. Farming is mechanized today, but it still requires muscle and sinew and strength. He was the kind of man you would want in a foxhole with you or in a dark alley. His two boys looked to be around eleven or twelve, and they watched nervously as their dad confronted me. His wife, still seated, held on to his hand. But what I noticed most of all were the tears glistening his eyes and the effort he made to control his voice. He was mad and sad all wrapped up into one.

"I am one season away from losing my farm, Mr. Bauer. It's been in our family for a hundred years. Nobody seems to care. We have been praying for a miracle. What can you do to help me?"

> **Farm families relearn every day that God is in control.**

Most farmers I met in Iowa and around the country have a strong religious faith. They deal with the wonder and the power of God's creation every day, and in the passing of each season, they see the mystery of life, death, and rebirth played out each year. It takes strong people to get up before dawn each day and work as hard as they can; all the while knowing that if the clouds dry up, or if the heat beats down, or if hail falls out of a spring sky a whole crop can be lost. Farm families relearn every day that God is in control.

I had read many agricultural briefing papers over the years in Washington—statistical analyses of declining farm populations and learned dissertations on the urbanization of America. I knew all the arguments about the market setting the price for a product and how many agricultural products can be produced cheaper in Mexico or on Canadian farms. I knew all the arguments against the old price-support programs and the practice of paying farmers to not grow a crop in order to keep supply down and prices up.

But all those words on paper seemed lifeless and irrelevant in front of real flesh and blood. This farm family had dreams like yours—a college education for their kids, a chance to retire and spend a little time together before "going home," maybe a chance for an occasional vacation, and the hope that a little money would be put aside for an emergency or to take care of an aging parent. Urban kids think hamburgers come from McDonald's. But America as a nation has never experienced the kind of famine and hunger that much of the world has. And for that we can thank the farm families like the one looking me in the eye on that hot summer morning in Iowa. They had been there for their country, and now this Iowa family wanted to know if anyone was going to be there for them.

Time and time again these hardworking men and women told me heartbreaking stories. Many of them were farming land that had been in their families for generations. They were the best farmers in the world, and they were producing record yields. But unlike the rest of America, the better they did their jobs the worse their economic condition became. They were cynical, and rightfully so. They had seen more than their share of politicians running for president who came into the state, hugged a hog, had their pictures taken on a farm, and were never seen again after they were elected. It took a lot to convince them I cared about more than just their vote.

Now, I know the farm crisis in America is due in part to worldwide trends in agriculture, but it is also due to deception and betrayal by the political establishment of our country.

When the Freedom to Farm Act was passed, Washington warned farmers that they would be losing some of the subsidies that helped support farm prices during bad years. Farmers would be more at risk in the marketplace. But in exchange for this risk, Washington politicians promised farmers that the government would fight harder to open up markets abroad to U.S. agricultural products. And they promised that a serious effort would be made to develop an income-insurance program to get farmers through the really bad years.

Instead, Washington did just the opposite. Our government stood by while China dumped billions of dollars of slave-made

But the bottom line was always the same. European governments fought for their farmers with passion and perseverance, while our political leadership made concession after concession.

goods into the United States at the same time they were buying fewer U.S. agricultural products. And in Europe, our "allies" come up with endless excuses to keep our products out, raising concerns from genetically engineered crops to growth hormones in the beef. But the bottom line is always the same. European governments fight for their farmers with passion and perseverance, while our political leadership make concession after concession.

And that isn't the only problem. Increasingly family farms are being bought up by large corporations that can mass produce and enjoy economics of scale. Near monopoly conditions in industries like meat packing result in farmers selling cattle for less than it costs to raise them. But I bet you didn't see the savings in the grocery store! The big farm corporations can spread the money around in Washington to make sure their interests are protected, while the family farmer can't even get to the right person in the bureaucracy.

And the unfair "death tax" results in thousands of farm families selling out after the breadwinner passes on. This trend, if left unaddressed, will lead to a dark day for the U.S. farmer and the consumer. If America wakes up one morning and discovers that the production and distribution of our food are controlled by a few large corporations, I guarantee we will regret it, and our food will cost more, not less. Just as important, we will have driven hundreds of thousands of our fellow Americans out of the livelihoods they love and that have nurtured their families for generations.

We went to war in Bosnia to save people with broken hearts, people forced off their land, without hope. But I faced families with broken hearts all through the rural communities of our country. American farmers live in what Washington derisively refers to as "flyover" country—places you look at out the window of your plane as you head somewhere else. Media elites are far from these families, and not many thousand-dollar-a-plate political fund-raisers are going to be held in the small towns across the Midwest and the South. The farm families that live in those places can't afford to pay a thousand dollars for dinner with a politician. They're too busy producing the food served at those dinners.

> Farm families . . . can't afford to pay a thousand dollars for dinner with a politician. They're too busy producing the food served at those dinners.

I believe in the free marketplace, but it is not perfect. The U.S. will lose an important part of the mosaic of American life if we lose the family farm. Farming is one of the last professions that enables parents and children to be together by working together. I believe the antitrust laws should be enforced against farm conglomerates, and that an income-insurance plan could help protect farmers during bad years. Washington should fight as hard to protect American farmers as other governments around the world do to protect theirs.

But these policy ideas only address part of the problem. The farmers I met in Iowa and throughout the country felt isolated and ignored. They were being left behind not only economically, but culturally too. It wasn't just the economic pressures that wore them down, but also a sense that small-town values were mocked by the cultural elites. These men and women still believe in the honor of a handshake and that a man's word is his bond. They exhibit a profound love of country, and they teach their children to love it too. I believe this is why there was a massive rejection of liberalism in rural communities all over the country in the 2000 presidential election. States like West Virginia, Tennessee, Arkansas, and Missouri were won by George Bush, largely because of support he received in rural counties.

The number of farm families in America continues to decline. As their numbers dwindle, fewer and fewer politicians will care about what happens to the family farm. I believe we must reach out our hand to these families, particularly in a time when we are running budget surpluses. We must do all we can to maintain their legacy. To forget them would be our loss.

CHAPTER 12

MEETING
MY FAMILY

Of all the families I met on the campaign trail, the one that had the biggest impact on me was my own! Don't get me wrong. My family has always been the center of my life. Even when I worked long days in the pressure of the Reagan White House as head of the Office of Policy Development, I would hurry home to have dinner with Carol and our children. Then after our kids were in bed, I'd head back to burn the midnight oil in the West Wing. School, basketball, gymnastics, soccer games, birthday parties, and dances have always been top priority. I was there when each of our children was born. OK, I admit it. I was reluctant at first. Carol said she wanted me to be in the delivery room, so I was there. But today, I thank God that I was. There is no better way to experience the miracle of life. In short, for Carol and me, nothing in this world ranks higher in priority than our kids.

And, of course, no one can know your children the way you do as a parent. You are there for their triumphs and defeats. While others sleep, you bathe them in tepid water in the middle of the night to bring down a fever. You comfort them when they don't win the game or when first love breaks their hearts. You celebrate with them when they bring home a good report card or win their first ribbon or trophy. You chase away the ghosts in the closet and under the bed. You applaud at the first recital and laugh with them when they tell a joke, even if you have heard it a thousand times. You are there when they enter the world, say their first word, take the first step; and you wave good-bye on their first day of

> **There are days when you are incredibly high, and days when your chin is bouncing off the floor. You laugh louder, cry harder, and find out in stark terms who your real friends are.**

college. But as well as Carol and I know our kids, nothing was more revealing than their behavior under fire, in the glare of lights and television cameras for fourteen long months. In short, as close-knit as we are, in the rigors of a presidential campaign I was able to meet them all over again.

Few things in life can compare to the emotional roller coaster of running for president. I guarantee you, this is one thing all the candidates would agree on. Governor Bush tried to keep his twin daughters out of the campaign for fear of the impact public attention and the natural nastiness of politics would have on them. Nasty and untrue things are said about you—nobody escapes unscathed. There are days when you are incredibly high, and days when your chin is bouncing off the floor. You laugh louder, cry harder, and find out in stark terms who your real friends are.

I am not complaining. If it were easy, everybody would do it. The competition for the most powerful position in the world is not for the faint of heart or the thin-skinned.

I've been in the political wars for years, and generally, I was prepared for what I knew would be a rough ride. In my time in D.C., I saw both true and untrue charges destroy political leaders. I watched Dan Quayle get skewered because of a misspelled word. I saw Richard Nixon leave town rather than risk the shame of likely impeachment. Judge Robert Bork was pilloried by enemies in the United States Senate. Justice Clarence Thomas was put through what he called "a high-tech lynching." He ultimately prevailed and now sits on the Supreme Court, but not before he and his family were put through hell. The smear campaign against him almost worked, and many people, including Christian and conservative leaders, abandoned him before it was over. Ronald Reagan fought charges for years that he was too dumb to be president, and the Iran-Contra scandal almost destroyed his presi-

> **Harry Truman was right. Washington, D.C., can be the kind of city where if you want a friend, you better buy a dog.**

dency. President Bush was accused of cocaine use, and his family has had to listen to constant jokes suggesting that he isn't bright. In South Carolina, calls were made to voters falsely charging that John McCain had illegitimate children—charges that were repeated even though they are patently untrue.

This smear campaign of a decent man and his family is one of the reasons I endorsed McCain. In addition, I became convinced after meeting with him privately that there was a better chance to get pro-life judges if McCain were elected. But my endorsement of McCain resulted in bitter personal attacks and charges that I had sold out. Nothing could be further from the truth.

I also faced attacks during the campaign that went to the very heart of what is most important to me: our marriage and the seriousness of the vows Carol and I made to each other. At one point in the campaign, I had to bring our whole family together for a press conference to answer unfounded charges of an affair. Don Imus, the radio shock jock, told millions of listeners that he "hoped the charges were true," because he would have had a field day with it on his irreverent radio show.

A former official of my own campaign was carted around by the staff of one of my rivals to major television and radio shows where he repeated the charges. Harry Truman was right. Washington, D.C., can be the kind of city where if you want a friend, you better buy a dog. Thank goodness we have two!

We survived. Of course, not one reporter could come up with any fact to prove the charges. We survived because the charges were untrue and the truth ultimately did prevail. The most anyone could come up with was that I had met with a trusted female staffer at campaign headquarters with my office door closed. Even many liberal reporters concluded the charges were ludicrous and another sign of the unnecessary nastiness of American politics. But it was an ordeal, nonetheless, and my family still bears the wounds of it today. (By the way, a candidate has to be able to meet privately with staff members. I solved the problem by putting a glass door on my office so that no one could speculate about what was going on. They could see everything with their own eyes.)

It is amazing that any normal family would voluntarily open themselves to the killing fields of American politics. Carol and I had prepared ourselves for the worst, but what about our children? How would they deal with the inevitable adversity?

If you have children, you know that each one is a unique individual created by God, with their own personality and characteristics. Our children are no exception. Yet each of them in their own ways were strong, resilient, faithful, loving, bold, and courageous in dealing with the slings and arrows that came our way.

SARAH

Let me start with Sarah, our middle child and younger daughter, who will appreciate that in this chapter she finally gets to go first! Of our three children, Sarah is the least interested in politics. She is a gentle soul who has a natural aversion to its nastiness and competitiveness. Sarah is a healer and uniter, and American politics is often about division and punches below the belt. She was the least enthusiastic about me running for office. On top of everything else, she began her freshman year in college in September 1999, right in the middle of my battle for the GOP nomination. The last thing she wanted was to be known as "Gary Bauer's daughter." (I won't keep you in suspense. She had nothing to worry about. When we visit her campus, I'm referred to as Sarah Bauer's dad!)

> **Sarah is a healer and uniter, and American politics is often about division and punches below the belt.**

When the untrue charges were made about me, charges that went to my marriage and my values, it was Sarah I worried about the most. When we decided to address the issue head-on by bringing the family together and holding a press conference to answer any questions, Sarah's worst fears were realized. Her dad was being skewered and unjustly accused, and she had to stand by and watch it. When we held the press conference, with a dozen cameras and fifty-plus reporters, I would have certainly understood if Sarah had given me a big "I told you so" and declined to fly home from college to join the rest of us. Instead she was a trooper, never complaining and always encouraging.

A few weeks later, after she had returned to college, I received a long letter from her. The envelope was simply addressed to "Dad," with our home address. I was in our den late one night after returning from another long campaign trip—five speeches a day with a dozen interviews interspersed between. I didn't know what was in the thick envelope but could tell from the handwriting on the outside that it was from Sarah. Here's what she wrote.

> Dad—
>
>   I know that this might be a little out of the ordinary, but this really has been weighing on my heart, so I knew that I had to write this and tell you what I have been feeling for the past couple of weeks and even months.
>
>   It was no secret that I was against the whole ordeal [the campaign]

from the beginning, afraid mainly for selfish reasons. But after having been gone at school and learning so much this past summer, I have come to respect you and your decision even more. Having the chance to step back and view life in the fast lane from a bystander's view has forced me to look at what you do, what you put up with, and what you face each and every day. In doing so I sigh, not because it hurts me personally, but because it hurts me to see how hard you are pushed and shoved, and how I am so unlike you in your strength, in that respect. I could never fight the fight that you have spent half your life preparing for. I could never take the blows that the opposition mercilessly throws at you. I could never have been so confident in the face of trials; but most importantly, I could never have been so successful in balancing all the acts you have come to master.

People ask me sometimes how it feels to have my dad run for president. Four months ago I may have humored them, told them surface experiences, and then asked to talk about something else. Since then, things have changed. Now I get questions and I am honest. Sometimes I am upset, sometimes I am scared, but for the most part I am proud. Never before have I been so confident in talking about it, and more satisfied in the fact that YOU are the one out there fighting. I need to be honest and tell you that this hasn't been easy. For me to get to the point of contentment in the situation has been a long time coming, but I know this is where I stand now. I bring it up in conversations on my own now, and people have been known to call me "daddy's girl." I smile, only because I would give so much to have half the traits you do that make you who you are. . . .

Dad, I wanted to write to tell you, from the bottom of my heart, that I love you. I wanted to write to let you know that you have my utmost respect and that I truly do back you up, not to fulfill an obligation, but a desire. Hang in there, Dad. There is not one day that goes by that I don't pray for you, think about you, and trust in you. I am proud to be able to say I have a dad strong enough in his convictions, sure enough in his vision, and confident enough in his faith to share it with a world that is in dire need. What a legacy you have, and what a job to live up to. I can only hope I am half as successful as you have been and will continue to be.

I love you, Sarah.

Wow! There's a letter I will be reading for the rest of my life. In fact, I pulled it out many times during the campaign when things weren't going well and I needed to be reminded what is really important. Sarah's heart right now is youth ministry. She wants to devote her life to working with America's kids. But whether she does that or something else, I know her big heart will make her a treasure anywhere she goes and whatever she does.

ELYSE

Our older daughter, Elyse, loves ministry too. But she has been pretty comfortable with politics over the years. In high school, she was selected for Girls State, an organization that trains young people in the political process, and did very well in an oratory contest sponsored by the American Legion. She graduated from the College of William and Mary in the spring of 1999 and couldn't wait to be part of the campaign. Elyse threw herself into the effort, working long hours at our campaign headquarters just outside Washington, D.C., and she eventually moved temporarily to Iowa, where she put together our youth campaign.

In no time, Elyse was giving speeches, debating representatives of the other campaigns, and doing television interviews as if she had been doing these things all her life. She found herself facing elected officials, candidate's siblings, seasoned political pros, and topnotch reporters, yet she came through with flying colors. In Iowa, I ended up doing better with the eighteen-to-twenty-four age bracket than with any other group. Walter Shapiro, a respected political columnist for *USA Today*, told me she was one of the most impressive people he met on the campaign trail.

As parents, it was incredible to see our firstborn enter the arena of life so confidently. For years, Elyse, Sarah, and Zachary had to sit and listen to my speeches. Now, in Iowa, I proudly listened to Elyse make the case for voting for me. She would end her speeches by telling audiences they could trust what I was saying because, she said, "He has been saying the same things at the dinner table for twenty years!" I had been, but most of the time I wondered if any of what I was saying was actually heard.

As I write this, Elyse is working for Congressman Frank Wolf, a highly respected member of Congress. Her passion for people and justice led her to work for a man leading the charge for human rights and religious liberty.

ZACHARY

Zachary was only twelve when the campaign began in earnest, and it was tougher for him to be directly involved. Carol and I wanted to keep his life as normal as possible, and that meant making sure he could stay in school and continue to participate in the sports he loves, soccer and basketball. One of his first questions was whether, if I won, we could continue to live in our own home rather than move to the White House. I told him I was pretty sure we would have to move, but he was relieved when I told him about the White House gym, bowling alley, movie theater, and the certainty that we could put up a basketball net in the White House driveway. At that point, I think visions of unique birthday sleepovers danced through his head. His soccer teammates cut to the chase and asked if the White House lawn could be their home field.

But I think I saw Zachary's heart the most when it became apparent that I would be dropping out of the race. When I didn't win the Iowa caucuses or the New Hampshire primary, it was obvious my under-dog candidacy wasn't going to suc-

> **In Zach's frustration, I saw his stalwart heart. I know that he is going to be a man who will fight the good fight, finish the race, and keep the faith.**

ceed. Running a real campaign costs thirty thousand dollars a day, or more, and we were heading toward campaign debts that I wanted to avoid. I thought Zach would be happy it was over. I had missed a lot of his basketball and soccer games, and now both his sisters were away from home. His life had been pretty disjointed for six months. But instead, he was mad. "Don't do it, Dad! Keep on fighting. You always tell me not to give up when my team is losing. Why are you giving up?" he wanted to know. There is nothing more humbling than to hear your own words quoted back to you by your children.

Zach doesn't like to lose, and neither do I. But there are times when reality has to be faced. I could not imagine a three-pointer at the buzzer that would put me in the lead. And since my campaign relied on other people's money, I had to be true to them when it was clear the race had narrowed down to two men who could get the nomina-tion, neither of whom was me.

But in Zach's frustration, I saw his stalwart heart. I know that he is going to be a man who will fight the good fight, finish the race, and keep the faith. Any team, on or off the court, will be fortunate to have him as a part of it. And I am glad he had the courage to challenge me and insist on consistency. Eventually, he understood my point about why it was time to call it quits, but he doesn't let a week go by without bringing up his hope that I'll run again.

There were no guarantees as to how our children would deal with the challenges of my race for the GOP nomination. They could have whined and complained and thought only of themselves. They could have become sullen or "turned off and tuned out." Instead, they rose to the occasion and gave me a glimpse of their futures. Thank you, guys— we love you all!

CAROL

Now, let me take a moment to say something about Carol. Her interest in politics goes way back. She was a Goldwater Girl in the 1964 campaign, a political-science major in college, and her first job out of college was with the Republican National Committee. We met there in 1970 while I was working part-time to put myself through law school. In short, Carol's longtime involvement in politics provided a perfect background to be a candidate's wife. There was one distinction, though. Until my campaign, Carol focused on issues, research, and the behind-the-scenes side of politics. As the wife of a candidate, she sometimes did her own speeches, radio or newspaper interviews, and other campaign events. I was delighted to see her enjoy the people side of politics. She often wondered aloud what it would be like to be the wife of a candidate if you didn't enjoy the public side of political life. Thank goodness that wasn't the case with her, but I must say that her observation has prompted me to look at any candidate's spouse with more empathy.

Carol saw as her first responsibility keeping the home fires burning, and she successfully retained a sense of family life in the midst of a chaotic year. We were able to travel together on occasion, and the family did a few great campaign bus trips across Iowa, New Hampshire, and Louisiana. She attended virtually all the presidential debates of which I was a part. But on most days, our time together was reduced to frequent phone calls. Carol had to deal with Zachary just as he was entering the turbulent teenage years, keep the house running smoothly, and do her monthly prayer alert for the Family Research Council, all the while having to read the daily attacks on me and, by extension, our family.

Every spare moment she had, Carol worked at the campaign headquarters, usually in the fund-raising area, and she worked hard to keep morale up. I know how tough that year was, but she seldom complained. I think she would have made a great First Lady, and perhaps she will get a chance in the years ahead. I thank God for my helpmate and the blessings we have enjoyed together.

One final note. I have met many people who have asked whether after months of exhausting campaigning that fell short of the nomination, my family and I would make the decision to run again. We have talked about it at length, and the answer is without hesitation, "Yes." I have devoted my entire life to the battle over ideas in America. I believe there is an obligation to repay our country, for America has given much. That is why I served my country for eight years with Ronald Reagan, why I turned down lucrative jobs with Washington law firms to build a center in Washington that represents America's average families, and why I am committed to defending the powerless, from unborn children to the average taxpayer. Other paths would have been easier, but I would not have slept well if I had taken the easy road instead of confronting the hard battle.

One of my great heroes, Teddy Roosevelt, said it best many years ago, and I carry his words in my billfold as a reminder.

> **I know how tough that year was, but [Carol] seldom complained. . . . I thank God for my helpmate and the blessings we have enjoyed together.**

It is not the critic who counts, not the man who points out how the strong man stumbled, or where the doer of deeds could have done better.

The credit belongs to the man who is actually in the arena; whose face is marred by dust and sweat and blood; who strives valiantly, who errs and comes short again and again; who knows the great enthusiasms, the great devotions, and spends himself in a worthy cause; who, at the best, knows in the end the triumph of high achievement; and who, at the worst, if he fails, at least fails while doing greatly, so that his place shall never be with those cold and timid souls who know neither victory nor defeat.

CHAPTER 13

THE CHALLENGE BEFORE US

I hope in these pages I have given you a sense of what it was like for a man with your values to run for the nomination of one of our two great parties to be president of the United States. It is easy to forget—amid all the polling, the focus groups, the talk shows, the late-night predictions, and television drama—that elections are remarkable and important matters. I was honored to be part of the 2000 campaign, though I did not on this try succeed. Nonetheless, I played a role in one of the more important things our nation does.

Elections are barometers of the American character. They test what we value, what we aspire to, what kind of people we are. This is the great wisdom of the American republic. It is built upon reflection and choice. It affirms the dignity and responsibility of all citizens to weigh, as equals under God, the principles upon which our shared way of life will rest. That is why it breaks my heart that so many Americans have dropped out of the political process, concluding that politics doesn't matter.

Why? Because there are important questions confronting us that will be settled in the political process. What is the American way of life today? What does it mean to be an American? What kind of society do we live in? In the days preceding the Civil War, Abraham Lincoln observed, with a sense of both tragedy and hope, that a "house divided against itself cannot stand." America today is a house divided. We are, on the one hand, practical and sensible, decent and charitable, creative and hardworking. We are, in many corners of the nation, a compassionate and prosperous people. Every day on the campaign trail I was reminded of these hopeful facts. We are still, at our best, a beacon of hope around the world, that "shining city on a hill" that draws to us all those yearning for freedom and peace.

But it would be foolish of me to tell you that all is well. In many ways we are also a nation that has lost the certainty of its purpose. We are a nation alienated from our own highest ideals. We love freedom, but too often we treat freedom as a blank check to live as we please, rather than a sacred responsibility to live just and virtuous lives. Too many Americans—from elementary-school children to college students to the CEOs of our largest corporations—do not know America well enough to love her deeply or criticize her wisely. Too many Americans take America for granted. Too many have abandoned the sacred duty to act as shepherds of the American idea. Too many of our sons and daughters tragically have never been taught what the American idea really is: that we are "One nation, under God, with liberty and justice for all"; that we are "endowed by our Creator" with certain "unalienable rights"; and that with those rights come inalienable responsibilities.

America is the wealthiest, most powerful nation in the world. This is the American age, the time in history for which America will be judged, for better or worse, and for all time. America has a greater reach around the world than any previous nation in recorded history. Our political ideas and popular culture reach into every nation. We have the opportunity to be an incredible force for good—for human liberty tempered by virtue, for the dignity of each person, and for the right of each individual to enjoy the fruits of his or her labor. An America with these values has been a beacon to enslaved peoples in every dark totalitarian nation on earth.

A former congressman tells the stirring story of seeing the influence of our country on the day when the people of Albania were able to vote freely for the first tine. The Berlin Wall had come down, and the sweet aroma of freedom was sweeping through Eastern Europe. All through the country people, including the aged and sick, lined up for hours at polling paces to patiently wait their turn. When the day drew to a close and voting ended, tens of thousands of people in the capital city gathered in a large public square, rather than go home. They couldn't quite believe they were now free, and many wanted to wait until the winners of the election were announced to confirm a fair election had taken place.

The crowd was so large it was impossible to see clearly the outer reaches of it, but suddenly from far in the back a chant began. It grew louder and louder, sweeping through the sea of humanity row by row. At first the chant was too far away to be clearly heard at the front of the crowd, but as it grew and moved it became clearer. The Albanians on the first day they could vote were chanting, "USA! USA! USA!" In some fundamental instinctive way, they understood that their liberty was directly related to our country and what we had stood for over the thirty-five years of the Cold War. This is the America that has stood for decency and on the side of right. When America exports the values of our Founding Fathers, ordered liberty under God, we are a force for great good.

But there are many things that call America into question, things that should sadden and disturb us: inner cities torn apart with violence, poverty, and a loss of hope; the weakening of the bond of marriage and the consequent rise of a culture of divorce; the drugging of millions of children on Ritalin and Prozac; a million and a half abortions a year and the sad promise of even more abortions to come, now that RU 486, the "abortion pill," has been approved for sale in the United States; and our popular culture, which makes a few media moguls rich at the expense of our most cherished values. We export that culture, with its images of gratuitous sex and violence. We are exporting a hedonism that undermines family values and virtue around the world.

From all sides there are claims that the American political system is

> **But America needs more than just political reform. America needs a reformation.**

broken and in need of reform—that special interests have too much power; elections have become media events about style, looks, and personality rather than substantive reflections on the nation and its future; narrow partisanship has replaced democratic self-government. All this is true. It is one of the reasons I believe we must more effectively regulate the influence of money in our politics or risk relegating average Americans to the back of the bus. But America needs more than just political reform. America needs a reformation. Without a restoration of our republican character, political reform will be impossible. Without reawakening to the ideals of the American founding, the great questions of our future—such as America's role in the post–Cold War world, human cloning, the role of the Supreme Court, the sacred bond between men, women, and children—will be decided by default by America's elite instead of by we the people.

If this is the way America goes, then America's best self will wither and be gone. "Our side" may win elections, but if we lose all the great issues that involve our humanity, the sacredness of life, and the need for virtue, political victories will be pointless.

WEALTH OR VIRTUE?

I still believe the Republican Party is the best hope for reviving American citizenship and self-government. That is why I have made my home in that party for all of my adult life. The Republican Party has a great tradition to stand on. It is the party of Lincoln and Reagan—and it is to their great legacy and example that the party and the nation must return.

Abraham Lincoln led the nation through its greatest crisis, the great Civil War over slavery. He understood the costs of freedom. He understood the price of defending human equality and dignity. He understood that politics requires compromise, but that some things are beyond compromise, and that the struggle of the nation is to live up to its own best principles.

> [Lincoln] **understood that politics requires compromise, but that some things are beyond compromise, and that the struggle of the nation is to live up to its own best principles.**

Ronald Reagan restored America's spirit at a time of great malaise. He reminded the nation, and declared to the world, that America is a great power because it is built on the moral idea of freedom under God. Reagan understood America, and so he understood that we could never compromise with the "evil empire" that was the Soviet Union. And because he understood the human thirst for liberty, he knew that the Soviet system would not last—if only America held fast as the great alternative.

Today's Republican Party is still the rightful heir to this great legacy of Lincoln and Reagan. But the party is divided over some fundamental issues. Conservatism is torn between two masters: wealth and virtue. The Republican Party in its platform has embraced the more traditional concept of liberty tempered by virtue. But its libertarian wing and many of the party's largest financial supporters require of it disarmament on the most important battles. The party will marshal all of its resources to argue for the privatization of Social Security or to fight for deregulation of multinational corporations, but many of its leaders grow faint of heart when making the case on issues of the heart and soul. And the emphasis by some in the party on trade, even over our own national security, is making the party that led the struggle in the Cold War sound more like the appeasers on the Left in the '70s and '80s.

Libertarian Republicans defend freedom primarily for its contributions to economic well-being, and because they believe individuals have a right to live as they please. To these Republicans, it is the bottom line that matters—the stock market, the national portfolio. Above all else, they are defenders of the wisdom of the marketplace. But the marketplace is not God, and if it is not tempered by virtue, it will demean our values and hasten our decline.

I want my party to believe, as I do, that business is a noble calling— especially for those who run small businesses, those who work hard every day, those who play by the rules and provide for their families. I have met these men and women all over the country: people who are creating the jobs, driving our economic growth, supporting church charitable groups, and defending family values. They believe that the nobility of enterprise is measured, above all, by its contribution to human dignity and virtue. I stand with them.

But we know that some big corporations prey on human virtue rather than embody it, and we are not afraid to criticize them when they do. We believe that trade must be judged not only according to its contributions to national wealth, but more importantly, by its contribution or threat to the national interest, to the ideals of American citizens, and to human rights around the world. The "virtue" Republicans are realistic enough to know the limitations of government. We've learned the hard lessons of experience from the many failures of the American welfare state. But we do not hate politics. We believe community service and public life can be as noble, honorable, and praiseworthy as life in the private sector. We believe, above all, that a nation is judged by the goodness of its people, not the size of its wallets, and that the mean-

> We believe, above all, that a nation is judged by the goodness of its people, not the size of its wallets, and that the meaning of freedom is not living as we please, but living with honor, reverence, and gratitude.

ing of freedom is not living as we please, but living with honor, reverence, and gratitude.

I am not saying that wealth and virtue are always in conflict. They are not. Wealth can be a virtue, as it allows us to defend our ideals, care for our families, and lift up those in need. But in the end, one must be more important than the other. We must choose one or the other, wealth or virtue, as the essence of the Republican Party and the essence of the nation. How we choose will shape America's destiny in the coming decades. Will we make goodness our first and highest principle or economic well-being? Will we aspire to a freedom that simply says, "Leave me alone to live as I please," or a freedom that says, "Give me the liberty to live a just life and the responsibility to help build a just and decent society"?

Looking back, Lincoln and Reagan both knew that prosperity alone was not enough to make America a great country. Their great wisdom—indeed, the mark of all great leaders—was to see what their respective ages demanded of them. Lincoln saw that America faced a great test to its ideals, one that required a tragic war and a hopeful restoration. Reagan saw that America needed to restore its strength and its values and that economic malaise threatened the American idea.

Today, America suffers from a moral malaise. The legacy of the Clinton years is a dark and shameful one: the corruption of our most sacred institutions, the undermining of our most sacred values. It is the legacy of "anything goes, nothing matters, different strokes for different folks, if it feels good do it," because there is nothing reliably right or wrong.

But it is not just in the realm of politics that our nation's values are being undermined. Some of our most powerful and successful industries have too often done much to undermine America, to lessen and dehumanize us. If the free marketplace is our highest value, we should praise the Hollywood moguls making millions with movies that exploit women and glamorize violence. We should welcome the casino to our neighborhood because it provides jobs. We should embrace the first biotech firm that clones a human being because it will make its stockholders rich. But all of these industries, even as they create wealth and provide a product the marketplace wants, undermine our virtue.

And so, a reformation requires a philosophy beyond just market capitalism. It requires a politics concerned again with virtue, a politics that can help lead America again to the better angels of its nature; a politics that reconnects American strength with American values. This is what the Republican Party should stand for. This is the project that lies before us.

THE CHOICES AHEAD

Once all the dust settled, the lingering fact is that the 2000 presidential election did very little to define and clarify the hard choices that will shape the American future. The Ping-Pong battle over "plans" and "lock boxes" and "surpluses" was not about insignificant things. But there was little or no real debate about the most significant things. There was no new thinking, no clear and reasonable appeal to the hearts and minds of the nation on the things that matter most or the hard challenges that lie just around the corner. We were called to no great cause and given no great goals.

Countless Americans I met, from the wealthiest businessman on Wall Street to the hardest working farmer, were prepared to do more for our country. Yet, in the entire presidential campaign, the first of the new century, not one candidate called on Americans to sacrifice for a purpose greater than their individual self-interest. Voters heard nothing but promises: I will lower your taxes; I will pay for your prescription drugs; I will improve your schools; I will increase your benefits; I will safeguard your rights.

John F. Kennedy exhorted us to, "Ask not what your country can do for you, but what you can do for your country." Ronald Reagan told us we had a rendezvous with destiny and an obligation to be the watchman on the tower of freedom. Their words invoked great causes and demanded of us stout hearts.

> **If people cannot be asked to consider the requirements of liberty when times are "good," when can they be asked?**

Perhaps this is the predictable politics in an era of a strong economy and no apparent major foreign political dangers that could disrupt the lives of average Americans. Or, perhaps it is a sign that those who would lead us are convinced the only way they can win is to pander to us. But a nation's life cannot prosper without hard choices any more than an individual's life can prosper without hard choices. And if people cannot be asked to consider the requirements of liberty when times are "good," when can they be asked? A nation that offers nothing more to its children than self-interest and material possessions will grow weak children, without an enduring love for the place of their birth. Ultimately, no one will be willing to lay down their lives for such a place and our lives will be about petty things that can be counted only on balance sheets. Nothing in the campaign prepared us for the great challenges just down the road.

What are these challenges? What are the issues of the future? What are the choices ahead? And does America have the political, moral, and civic coinstitution, the strength of character and steadiness of leadership, to make good choices and to restore America to its highest principle?

Looking around, it is hard not to be impressed with all the cutting-edge inventions, the technologies, and the mass prosperity that American ingenuity has created. From cell phones to blood-pressure medications to electronic commerce to virtual-reality entertainment, in no society in history have more people had more tools; and never before have the tools been so remarkable, so useful, and so seductive. You can walk down the street of an American city and get stock quotes on your cellular phone. A satellite system can track your car and give you directions if you get lost. The Christmas catalogs this year advertised robotic dogs.

But it is hard to ignore the downsides of the new technological capitalism. We have become a society of images and entertainment. We read less and know less. Children spend, on average, four to five hours a day sitting passively in front of television screens and video games, watching shows that too often belittle religion and family—shows that glorify loveless sex, adults behaving like adolescents, and gratuitous violence.

Even our most powerful, most respected companies have entered the least respectable businesses. A recent story in the *New York Times* chronicled the largest sellers of hard-core pornography. The winners will surprise and shock you: General Motors, which owns the satellite television company DirecTV, sells more than $200 million a year in pay-per-view "sex films"; AT&T Corporation owns a hard-core pornography channel called the Hot Network, which shows "real, live all-American sex—not simulated by actors." Many other mainstream companies do large amounts of business in the pornography industry. But none of their corporate leaders was willing to speak publicly about this side of their businesses.[1]

What does this say? First, it says that shame is not completely dead in America. These corporate giants know that main-street American citizens, if they knew what these companies were selling, would be outraged. Second, it says that these companies can get away with doing

> **As a matter of public policy and public morality, we have lost the will or moral sense to put limits on activities that undermine American culture and American values.**

what they do. Third, it says that while shame is not dead, there is a large market for material that lessens and cheapens our humanity. It means that as a matter of public policy and public morality, we have lost the will or moral sense to put limits on activities that undermine American culture and American values.

It is easy to say that popular culture doesn't matter or that one person's obscenity is another person's art. But to do so, in the end, cheapens our humanity. It makes sex meaningless and devalues the commitment to marriage. It demeans life and makes everything profane, destroying our moral sense and therefore our capacity for reverence, self-restraint, and sacrifice.

The age of technology has given us many things—cures for diseases, comforts and conveniences, the capacity for exploration. But there is, around the corner, a series of technological revolutions that will test our sense of what it means to be human. Genetic screening of human embryos will allow us to know what our children will look like and what disabilities they might have. Will we be able to resist the temptation to pick and choose what we like and abort what we don't? Stem-cell research promises cures to many common diseases. But it depends for its advance on a ready supply of human embryos. Is this what we want—an entire medical industry that depends on the buying and selling of human life? Soon human cloning may go from science fiction to real-life possibility. Is this what we want—the capacity to clone ourselves, to manipulate human nature to any ends we see fit, to give those who love power the capacity to control human destiny through science? In short, do we want to play God?

Two biotech companies announced near the end of the campaign that they had fertilized a pig's egg with nuclei of cells from a human being. The "pig-man," as one observer called it, was permitted to grow to a thirty-two-cell embryo before it was destroyed in the laboratory. Some researchers suggested the purpose of this experiment was to eventually

> **Shouldn't a free people have a chance to discuss the implications and make decisions about whether a just and decent society can permit such a thing?**

create a subhuman creature that could be used for medical and scientific research.[2] Sound far-fetched or far, far away? Perhaps. But who would have guessed in 1980 that before the century was over we would be growing human embryos in order to harvest stem cells to treat illnesses in other individuals. And, that this would happen without citizens having an opportunity to have a say.

Science races madly ahead. Can anything be done about it? Should anything be done about it? Shouldn't a free people have a chance to discuss the implications and make decisions about whether a just and decent society can permit such a thing? Or does our future rely on whether scientists have the moral code to restrain themselves?

Are our politics up to the challenge? The signs are not good. It was virtually impossible in the 2000 campaign to have a legitimate debate on the FDA's approval of RU 486. For the first time in the history of the FDA, it has approved a drug whose purpose is not to heal or save life, but to destroy inconvenient life. We approved a pesticide for humans, but neither candidate really wanted to debate this issue. I hope that now, with a change of government, this decision can still be reviewed and reversed.

To resist these temptations—to choose reverence instead of power, dignity instead of manipulation, wonder instead of control, responsibility instead of absolute autonomy, God instead of man—requires a moral wisdom and largeness of spirit that our culture and politics now lack. Today, this hollowness of soul is evident in the mercenary capitalism of our corrupt popular culture. Tomorrow, if we don't choose a different path, if we don't rebuild our culture and our politics, it may become even more dangerously evident in the mercenary capitalism of those who manipulate and corrupt human life for profit.

We need to—we must— choose a different path. The essence of conservatism must be not unbridled capitalism but the preservation and restoration of the values that give life its meaning, purpose, and dignity. Our conservative agenda must be more than just an attack on government bureaucracy. We must be careful not to undermine our own governing institutions in the name of freedom.

> **The essence of conservatism must be not unbridled capitalism but the preservation and restoration of the values that give life its meaning, purpose, and dignity.**

It is true that government overreach has at times hurt—and hurt seriously—the fabric of our society. But what we need today is to restore our institutions, not to run against them or vilify them. We need to restore limited government, while at the same time restoring the nobility and reverence of public life. We need to recognize that democracy has a role in restraining the moral excesses of capitalism, that politics has a role in reconnecting American prosperity to our most cherished values.

My party has serious matters to deal with, but what about the other guys? The Democratic Party has always claimed to defend those most in need—which is, at its best, the noblest human impulse: charity. That is why hardworking blue-collar Americans like my parents are proud members of that party. Democrats seek to defend the environment in the name of reverence for the natural world, another noble goal. And yet, the majority of Democrats abandon reverence when it comes to the mystery of life. They passionately defend abortion on demand and so devalue reverence for life, which devalues the very basis for taking responsibility for the poor. They claim to care about America's most disenfranchised communities. And yet the biggest roadblock to extending the American dream to those unfairly left behind is the decline of the family—especially the dereliction of many inner-city fathers and the astronomical rates of illegitimacy. But the fact is that the cultural left has done everything possible to undermine the family: defending sexual freedom, handing out condoms to teenagers, and defending a sex-filled popular culture in the name of freedom of speech and artistic expression. The party of Harry Truman and FDR has made a devil's pact with those who argue that America means nothing bigger than the right to do whatever you want if it brings you pleasure. At the 2000 Democratic convention, a Boy Scout honor guard was booed by delegates who could not tolerate that organization's sensible resistance to putting homosexual men in charge of young boys. Millions of Democrats care about heartland values. I have met them and talked with them all over America. In November of 2000, they left their party and put states like West Virginia, Missouri, Tennessee, and Arkansas into the Republican column. Does the national Democratic party really want its historic legacy to be abortion on demand, same-sex marriage, and an elite hostility to the most deeply held faith beliefs of millions of Americans?

THE AMERICAN FUTURE

In the coming decade, there will be a serious debate about what America is, what citizenship is, what we aspire to as a nation. This debate will not center on the size of government but on the role of government. It will not center on making America more prosperous but on making a prosperous America more virtuous. Neither contemporary conservatism nor contemporary liberalism is fully ready for this challenge.

We need a new politics: a politics that knows the limits of government but also reveres government as a noble institution, a politics that reaches out to those in need without accepting the welfare-state policies that undermine American values. We need a politics that has no illusions of creating a perfect society, but aspires to something greater than a blind, uncaring, reactionary libertarianism.

> **We need a politics that is, as the old saying goes, "not afraid to speak truth to power."**

We need a politics that is, as the old saying goes, "not afraid to speak truth to power."

America in the third millennium faces a choice: Will we turn inward, caring only for the size of our bank accounts, losing our souls in virtual experiences, forgetting the American idea that makes all our freedoms possible? Or will we make America again a great nation with the courage and the will to preserve its principles at home and defend its ideals abroad?

The American spirit is strong, even if it wavers amid the great temptations of a hollowed-out influence. The American idea is strong, because it is built not merely on human invention but on self-evident truths that transcend human design. The next century can be, like the last one, an American century, but only if we return to the first principles that give America its strength. This is our challenge, our noble calling. Providence is still on our side. I believe it is. I believe that if we hear the call to citizenship once again, a great American awakening is not only possible, it is our destiny.

AFTERWORD

On February 4, 2000, Carol and I and our children headed to the National Press Club to announce that I would be withdrawing from the race for the Republican presidential nomination. It was a bittersweet day. We were exhausted and bruised and looking forward to some normal days again. But we were also sad that the great adventure of the previous year was drawing to a close. Many of our supporters around the country were urging me to stay in the race, but campaigning is very costly and we had already gone into debt. It was time to face the situation and move on to fight another day.

The pressroom was packed with many of the Washington, D.C., reporters who had been covering the race. C-Span televised my statement live, and the other networks had their cameras there as well. After the press conference was over, many reporters came up to us to say that they thought I had run an honorable campaign that raised serious issues.

I feel it is fitting to close this book with the last statement I made as a candidate in 2000. Please consider it my pledge to you that I will continue to fight the good fight, finish the race, and keep the faith.

Friday, February 4, 2000

FOR IMMEDIATE RELEASE

Twelve months ago I stepped into the area of presidential politics, to dare greatly, to undertake a worthy cause. Not because I was certain of victory—far from it—but because of my devotion to what Roosevelt called "great enthusiasms."

The greatest of these is our noble American experiment in self-government. I believed then, and believe now, that I have a governing vision for our country, a vision rooted in faith that America truly is, as Abraham Lincoln once noted, "the last, best hope of earth."

Lincoln's prophetic vision of America's indispensable place on the world stage has been fulfilled in part. Twice in the twentieth century, when the survival of civilization itself hung in the balance, America shouldered the burden of freedom's defense. Our nation sent its husbands and fathers, brothers and sons to die on foreign shores from Normandy and Iwo Jima to Pork Chop Hill and Khe Sanh, that the world might enjoy, in Lincoln's words, "a new birth of freedom." At enormous cost in blood and treasure, we defeated the twin evils of Nazism and Communism. As we now look forward into a new century, our vision of free, self-governing people prevails across the globe, where once tyranny and despotism ruled with iron fist. The power of brute force succumbed to the power of an idea.

Four centuries ago, our Puritan forefathers stood on the Atlantic shore, looked westward into the howling wilderness and envisioned a "shining city on a hill," a beacon to the world. The destiny they imagined has been largely fulfilled. Our founders boldly proclaimed to the world a distinctly American faith, a faith rooted in the self-evident truths that "all men are created equal and endowed by their Creator with certain unalienable rights, that among these are life, liberty and the pursuit of happiness." Today, Lady Liberty lifts her lamp beside the golden door and freedom enlightens the world.

I decided to run for president because I believe our American destiny is in jeopardy. It is in jeopardy because we have, for the second time in our history, excluded an entire class of human beings from the unalienable rights with which we all have been endowed by

God, the author of liberty. Our courts have excluded the unborn from the first of all rights, the right to life. Like a pebble tossed into a pool, the insidious consequences of *Roe v. Wade*'s devaluation of human life have rippled throughout our culture, coarsening and debasing it. This will stick in our throats until we make it right, until we welcome all our children into the world and protect them in law. Widening the circle of liberty to include the unborn will be the great civil-rights struggle of the twenty-first century.

On this I will not be moved; on this I will not go away.

Secondly, our American destiny is in jeopardy from a policy toward Communist China that is potentially leading our country to disaster. The trade wings of both political parties have placed commercial interests before our historic national commitment to the expansion of human rights and even our own national security. Tempted by the allure of the "China market" and seduced by the promise of easy profits, we have turned a blind eye to the massive Communist assault on human rights and dignity. We have willfully chosen to ignore China's massive arms buildup and increasing belligerence toward our allies in Asia, in particular a free and democratic Taiwan. The current policy can only be characterized as one of appeasement.

Though I would not for a moment presume to compare myself to Winston Churchill, I would remind you of how that great man raised a lonely yet thunderous voice first against the growing threat of Nazism, and subsequently against Soviet Communism. Reviled as a warmonger, in both instances Churchill was vindicated and the West prevailed over the forces of darkness, but at horrific cost.

Ronald Reagan, whom I had the great honor to serve in the White House, was ridiculed when he suggested that the world could not long remain half slave and half free, that the appeasers of tyrants were wrong and our goal in the Cold War should be victory over

Soviet Communism. Today, a piece of the Berlin Wall stands on the mantle of that good man's fireplace out in California.

I neither seek nor desire a new Cold War with China. But the appeasers in my party are wrong. We are courting disaster in an attempt to placate China's Communist rulers by opening our market and shepherding them into international trade organizations. To propose "normal trade relations" with China is repugnant both to our national security and the universality of God-bestowed human rights.

On this I will not be moved; on this I will not be silent.

Finally, we must ask ourselves from whence comes our wealth? Is our wealth to be found in our stock portfolios, in our gross domestic product or growing mutual fund retirement accounts? Is our wealth to be measured solely by the Dow Jones Average or today's rise in the NASDAQ exchange?

I would not for a moment demean our material prosperity. It is astounding, unprecedented in human history, and the envy of the world. But I believe our true wealth is to be found in our ideals and in our families. Our true wealth derives from lovingly packed lunchboxes and prayers around the dinner table. Our true wealth derives from the strength of our most important institutions—marriage and the family.

Yet these, too, are at risk. Our courts are redefining marriage in such grotesque ways as to make it unrecognizable. Unless this is stopped, our courts, against the sovereign will of the people, soon will redefine marriage to permit men to marry men and women to marry women.

Government, moreover, imposes a crushing tax burden on the family, driving mothers from the home and making two-income households a necessity.

The institution of marriage and family, tested by four thousand years of Judeo-Christian tradition, is the bedrock on which our civilization stands. We tinker and experiment with them at unimaginable risk to our posterity.

This is why we must stand in defense of family and marriage against those who would redefine them in novel and bizarre ways. And this is why we need a tax code that is family friendly and which values our human capital as highly as our material wealth.

On this I will not be moved; on this I will not go away.

Today, I am bowing out of the race for the presidency. I willingly accept the verdict of the voters. I thank the good people of Iowa and New Hampshire and all those who share my governing vision for America's future and who supported my candidacy with their prayers and contributions. I congratulate my worthy Republican opponents and wish them well.

Though I am leaving the race, I am not leaving the arena. I intend to carry on the fight for those things I have mentioned today: a renewed respect for life, a China policy rooted in our American ideals and not appeasement, and a government that is friendly to marriage and the family. If we do these things, this new century can be another American century, and we will ensure that our nation remains the shining city on a hill our forefathers envisioned.

NOTES

CHAPTER TWO: THE DAY AFTER COLUMBINE

1. Testimony of Darrell Scott before the House Judiciary Sub-committee on Crime, 27 May 1999.

2. Lindsey Layton, "Prayer and Punishment," *Washington Post*, 28 May 1999, A-1.

CHAPTER THREE: WE HOLD THESE TRUTHS

1. Lori Yaklen, "Tear Down This Wall," *Washington Times*, 20 November 2000, A-23.

CHAPTER FOUR: BABY HOPE

1. "Abortion Opponents Promise Renewed Legislative Effort," Associated Press, 20 April 1999.

2. David S. Oderberg, "A Messenger of Death at Princeton," *Washington Times*, 30 June 1998, A-17.

CHAPTER FIVE: DUTY, HONOR, COUNTRY

1. Thomas E. Ricks and Steve Vogel, "USS *Cole* Guards Told Not to Fire First Shot," *Washington Post*, 14 November 2000, A-1.

CHAPTER SIX: RELIGIOUS PERSECUTION

1. Wesley Pruden, "A Lonely Passion for Religious Rights," *Washington Times*, 20 October 2000, A-4.

2. Lorie Montgomery, "Emotions Help Shape China Debate," *Washington Post*, 24 May 2000, A-15.

3. Testimony of Gao Xiao Duan, Planned Birth Officer, before the Subcommittee on International Operations and Human Rights of the Government Reform and Oversight Committee of the U.S. House of Representatives, 10 June 1998.

4. Ibid.

5. Testimony of Zhou Shau Yon before the Subcommittee on International Operations and Human Rights of the Government Reform and Oversight Committee of the U.S. House of Representatives, 10 June 1998.

6. Seth Faison, "Dissident Imprudently Ridiculed Harsh Rule," *New York Times*, 17 November 1997.

7. John Pomfret, "U.S. Now a Threat in China's Eyes," *Washington Post*, 15 November 2000, A01.

CHAPTER SEVEN: HOSTILITY TO FAITH

1. Editorial, "The Piety Parade," *L.A. Times*, 20 December 1999, Metro Section.

CHAPTER EIGHT: CYNICISM

1. C. William Pollard, *The Soul of the Firm* (NY: Harper Business; Grand Rapids, Mich.: Zondervan Publishing House, 1996).

2. Maureen Dowd, "Playing the Jesus Card," *New York Times*, 16 December 1999.

CHAPTER TEN: THE ELDERLY

1. Martin Cross, "The $6 Trillion Surplus Heist," *Washington Times*, 1 November 2000.

CHAPTER THIRTEEN: THE CHALLENGE BEFORE US

1. Timothy Egan, "Selling Pornography Becoming Big Business,: *Cleveland Plain Dealer*, 27 October 2000, p. E1.

2. Jay Bottum, "The Pig Man Cometh," *Weekly Standard*, 23 October 2000, p. 18.

ABOUT THE AUTHOR

GARY L. BAUER campaigned for the Republican presidential nomination in 2000 and brought the conservative pro-family, pro-life philosophy to the forefront in seven nationally televised debates. Prior to running for president, Mr. Bauer served for eleven years as president of *the Family Research Council* in Washington, D.C. President Ronald Reagan appointed him to the position of Undersecretary of Education and Director of the Office of Policy Development in the Reagan White House. He has authored *Our Journey Home, Our Hopes-Our-Dreams* and coauthored *Children at Risk*. He and his wife, Carol, have three children.

Currently, Mr. Bauer is president of *American Values*, a nonprofit policy group in Washington, D.C., dedicated to promoting pro-life, pro-family, pro-small business and conservative causes centered on family, faith, and freedom nationally and around the world.

Mr. Bauer is also the founder and chairman of the *Campaign for Working Families* (CWF), a political action committee dedicated to electing pro-family, pro-life candidates to public office and to defending traditional values at the ballot box. Since its inception, CWF has raised nearly $10 million and financially supported over three hundred conservative candidates for state and federal office. Over 70 percent of CWF's candidates have won their races. CWF has also supported ballot initiatives designed to protect the sanctity of marriage and promote family values in half a dozen states. With nearly 100,000 members, the

Campaign for Working Families is one of America's preeminent political action committees.

To learn more about Gary L. Bauer visit the web sites:

www.garybauer.com

www.cwfpac.com

–or–

Mail Form To:
Gary L. Bauer
2800 Shirlington Road, 6th Floor
Arlington, VA 22206

I would like to know more about: ____ *American Values*
                                   ____ Campaign For Working Families

Please mail information to me at:
Name _____
Street _____
City _____ State _____ Zip _____
E-mail address _____
